THE ELEPHANT WALK
COOKBOOK

THE ELEPHANT WALK
COOKBOOK

Cambodian Cuisine from the
Nationally Acclaimed Restaurant

Longteine De Monteiro
and
Katherine Neustadt

FOOD PHOTOGRAPHS BY
ALAN RICHARDSON

INGREDIENT PHOTOGRAPHS BY
ALAN RICHARDSON AND ANTONIS ACHILLEOS

TRAVEL PHOTOGRAPHS BY
KATHERINE NEUSTADT AND BOB PERRY

ILLUSTRATIONS BY ALAN WITSCHONKE

Houghton Mifflin Company

Boston   New York

1998

Library of Congress Cataloging-in-Publication Data

De Monteiro, Longteine.
The Elephant Walk cookbook : Cambodian cuisine from the
nationally acclaimed restaurant / Longteine De Monteiro
and Katherine Neustadt ; photographs by Alan Richardson.
p. cm.
Includes index.
I S B N 0-395-89253-8
1. Cookery, Cambodian.   2. Elephant Walk (Restaurant)
I. Neustadt, Katherine.   II. Title.
TX724.5.C16D4 1998
641.59596 — dc21
98-28214 CIP

Travel photographs:
Bob Perry: pages 3, 12, 16, 18, 21, 23, 25, 28, 32, 39, 125, 177, 201, 261
Katherine Neustadt: pages 4, 6, 8, 11, 15, 17, 19, 22, 26, 30, 35, 69, 103, 155, 177, 225, 249.

Cover photograph: Classic Noodle Soup (*K'tieu*), page 78.

PRINTED IN THE UNITED STATES OF AMERICA

DOS 10 9 8 7 6 5 4 3 2 1

FOR MY MOTHER AND FATHER
— L.D.M.

ACKNOWLEDGMENTS

When I look back to the very beginning of The Elephant Walk, I see a lot of high hopes and dreams and a few key people who helped them come to life. Our landlord in Somerville, Don Warner, saw something special in our venture that he was willing to support, which allowed us to open our first restaurant with less capital and backing than was probably advisable. Nancy Harmon Jenkins, a Somerville neighbor and food celebrity in her own right, visited The Elephant Walk shortly after we opened and has been its guardian angel ever since, taking us under her wing, getting us reviewed in the *New York Times* and generally making us feel welcome and appreciated. It was Nancy who brought both Doe Coover and Kathy Neustadt to this project, two people whose skills, patience and good humor have contributed critically and delightfully to the making of this book.

The greatest measure of support and contributions has come from my own family members, who have lived and breathed The Elephant Walk for so long that it's amazing we don't all have trunks. To each and every one of them—my husband, Ken; my daughters, Launa and Nadsa; and my sons-in-law, Gérard Lopez and Bob Perry—I owe the deepest gratitude and love for their talents, hard work and, most especially, their willingness to travel with me on this path.

—Longteine (Nyep) De Monteiro

As one who has felt especially honored to have been brought along for part of the journey, I can only add that the work of channeling for Nyep—as we jokingly refer to it—has been a source of true pleasure for me. To have the opportunity to share and learn so much from her and then to get first crack at her food has been an amazing gift—I must have done something very right in a past life.

I also want to say a word of thanks to my own family, who, in various ways and with mouths open and closed, have supported me in this work. To Casey and Nick and Bill, particularly, my love and heartfelt thanks.

—Kathy Neustadt

AUTHORS' NOTE

In order to avoid encumbering the recipes with special notes that would have to be repeated, we have gathered together all the information about ingredients in the Glossary (page 283). Entries are listed there in alphabetical order just as they appear in the recipes—under "unsweetened coconut milk" rather than under "coconut milk," for example—and include a description of the ingredient, how to use it, where to find it and what to substitute for it.

Contents

THE ELEPHANT WALK
COOKBOOK

INTRODUCTION

The story behind *The Elephant Walk Cookbook* is as much a personal journey as it as a culinary one. In retrospect, I can see where the two have been intertwined throughout my entire life. I never set out to be a chef — or a restaurateur, for that matter — but it seems that this is what was intended for me. The stolen hours and meals in the kitchen with the servants when I was a child, the difficult task of cooking for my father when I was a young woman, my role as a diplomat's wife and hostess and — most dramatic and clear — my decision at midlife to turn cooking into a source of support for our family in exile in France: I can now look back on all of these events and see the thread, gradually growing into a cord, that has tied my life to food.

I was born into an upper-class Cambodian, or Khmer, family in the capital city of Phnom Penh. My father, who had studied in Vietnam and received his advanced training under the French system of education there, returned to Cambodia to become the country's first veterinarian, a position of considerable importance and prestige, which kept him in constant touch with foreign colleagues and new ideas. As a Cambodian woman, my mother's experiences were more traditional, and it was her job to oversee the duties of the home, which were considerable, as the family grew to include eight children.

We had lots of servants living with us as I was growing up: a couple of cooks, two or three kitchen helpers, a few house cleaners and a few gardeners, whose labors regularly provided food for the table. Sometimes I am amazed when I think of the number of people who worked in our kitchen (like a small restaurant staff, really), but then I remember how many mouths there were to feed and all that had to be done by hand: the constant, physically demanding, time-consuming work that went into preserving fish, making coconut milk, grinding spice powders, slicing bamboo shoots, roasting eggplant and on and on, several times a day. Meals for the large number of people living in our family compound were a major production.

From the time I was little, I was drawn to the world of the kitchen, not so much as a place to learn to cook properly — which is what my mother wanted me to do there — but as a place to explore exciting new foods. In the heat of the day, when my parents would nap, I loved to go downstairs and play in the kitchen, where the servants would be cooking their midday meal and would let me help. Looking back on it now, it seems like such an inauspicious, but natural, beginning for a career in food, though I never would have dreamed it at the time.

The servants cooked different foods for themselves from what they made for my parents, and I loved that — it was very exciting to me. For example, they made a dish called *Somlah Kako*, which we serve at our restaurant and which I've included in this book. It's a simple, basic dish, a Cambodian ratatouille that uses green papaya, eggplant, string beans, spinach and a small fresh river fish, or sometimes chicken. To this, the servants would add lots of strong flavors, like preserved fish and chilies, to make the dish go further — to make the food taste like more even when they were working with less — and I found it delicious. The difference between what the servants ate and the more subtle, restrained versions that my family ate intrigued me, and the stronger flavors of the kitchen captivated me.

Another really special combination was *prahok*, the intensely flavored paste made from preserved fish that I was used to only as a seasoning, chopped up with lime juice, a little bit of sugar and a lot of chilies. Then the cooks would pick green papayas, some star fruit and a lot of other unripened fruits that were very acidic and sour, slice them and dip them in the *prahok* sauce. It was wonderful. You have to keep in mind that for Cambodian people of refined taste, like my own family, it was unthinkable — disgusting, even — to eat uncooked *prahok*, and here I was heartily lapping it up while the rest of the household slept. My recollection of the flavors, infused with the secretiveness of the whole scene, makes this one of my best childhood memories.

The garden around our house offered another taste of paradise for me. There were fruit trees of every sort: coconut palms, jackfruit, longan, papayas, bananas, star fruit, some jujubes and a few pomelos — all ripe (and unripe) for the picking. I can remember lying in bed in the morning and hearing my mother's voice in the garden. She used to rise early and go out with the servants to oversee the trimming of the trees, the

gathering of fruit from high up in the branches or other cleanup work. She would also walk among her herb plants to collect what she needed for the next meal, digging up ginger, galangal — a root that resembles ginger — and fresh turmeric or, perhaps, cutting stalks of lemongrass and sprigs of cilantro.

My mother not only watched over the work of the kitchen staff, but also did some cooking herself, and when she did, she wanted me at her side. She would always say, "Come on, Nyep" — that's my nickname, it means something like "sweet little thing" — "you have to watch this so that when you grow up, you'll know how to do it." It was all about learning to be a good housewife, and I wasn't very interested in that at the time, so I was a bad student. But anything having to do with food has always seemed to come easily to me, so I absorbed it all anyway, without meaning to. My mother would say to me, "In this dish, you put this, but don't put that," and even though I wasn't paying attention, I seemed to collect it all in my head. My mother isn't alive anymore, but I can still remember her lessons.

My father also played a big role in my life when it came to food. While living in Vietnam, in Hanoi, during the 1920s, he was exposed not only to the French education system, but also to everything else *haute classe,* and it marked him for life. To begin with, it was a time when few Cambodians except for royalty traveled, let alone studied, abroad, so that set him apart. Perhaps that's why he became so deeply influenced by French culture. He was very European, my father, very French in the way he thought, the way he talked, even in the way he raised his children.

From the outside, I think other Cambodian people thought it was strange; they talked about him, saying that he was Catholic, like the French, which he wasn't. But he did deal mostly with French people professionally, and they respected him a lot. At home, when we were little, he made us practice French. He made his children ask him in French, "Papa, please give me one banana." Because he started us off at home learning French this way, by the time we got to school, it really wasn't difficult.

The extent of the French influence in my father's life showed up in dramatic form in his diet: he ate only French food. Lunch and dinner, every day: French food. My family was unique in Phnom Penh — probably in all of Cambodia — because none of the other Cambodian families ate French food at home. Ever. Except for the bread, French food didn't really penetrate Khmer cuisine. People would, on occasion, go to one of the French restaurants run by the ethnic Chinese that catered to the French provincial rulers and the Khmer upper class, but they didn't cook French food in their own kitchens.

My father, on the other hand, never went to a restaurant and expected to eat his French food at home every day. I don't know why my father loved it so much; sometimes I think he must have been French in a past life.

My father sent my brothers and my older sister off to France to be educated while I became what we would jokingly call a "home student," which actually meant learning to cook for my father. Up until that time, my mother had been struggling alone to produce *haute cuisine* at the same time that she watched over the servants, who were preparing Cam-

bodian food for the rest of the family. I can remember my mother making pâté when I was very young; she also made cheese and butter from the fresh milk that was always on hand because my father was a veterinarian. We thought it was a great feast when she made her own mayonnaise to serve with fresh fish or freshwater lobster, though I'm sure it was a great puzzlement to the rest of our community.

Cooking French food was hard for my mother. My father had bought her an enormous French cookbook called *Je Sais Cuisiner*, which he expected her to use, but she didn't read French and wasn't particularly fond of the taste of the food. Sometimes she would run out of ideas and would have to order food from one of the French restaurants in the city (to this day, I can still remember some of the names of the dishes). Then she'd bring it home and serve it to my father — it was a lot to handle alone.

So I decided to try to help my mother by taking over this responsibility, and when I was 17, the French cookbook became mine. My father not only wanted his food to taste just right, but he expected the presentation to be good as well. Otherwise, he wouldn't touch it. *"Saloperie"* — slop — he would say and push it away. Sometimes I would cry. I'd worked hard, and I would be so disappointed in myself. My father was really tough, but I thank him for it. Now that I know the demands of the restaurant business, I see that I couldn't have gotten any better training.

I suppose that all this exposure to different kinds of cooking at an early age gave me a heightened awareness, so that I picked up little bits of information about what people were eating everywhere I went. When I traveled with my father, my horizons broadened beyond the two kinds of food that came out of our kitchen. When we visited the coast, for example, I was struck by the prevalence of sea fish and the influence of Chinese taste; along the country's borders, I learned to recognize the distinctive flavors of Thai, Vietnamese and Lao cuisines; in the cities, I saw the country's elite dine on French and aristocratic Thai food.

When I was 18, my parents arranged a marriage for me with a very promising young man, Kenthao De Monteiro, who was a minister in the Cambodian Parliament. De Monteiro was the name of a sixteenth-century Portuguese visitor to the country, and his descendants had gone on to become quite distinguished. These included at least one physician, one adviser and one prime minister to various Cambodian kings (this last one was so famous, a street in Phnom Penh is named after him).

In his early twenties, Kenthao had been sent to Paris to study with a handful of other promising Cambodian students (one of them, strangely enough, was Saloth Sar, who would later become known to the world as Pol Pot, murderous leader of the Khmer Rouge). There he had earned degrees in literature, political science and, finally, law from the Sorbonne. Shortly after his return to Cambodia, he was made a judge, and by the time I met him, he had been elected to the Cambodian Congress, where he later served as Minister of National Education and Vice-President of the National Assembly.

After his career in Cambodia's internal political scene, Ken joined the diplomatic service, and we began to travel as a family, with our daughters, Launa and Nadsa. In each new country where we were stationed — first in the Philippines, then Yugoslavia and, finally, in Taiwan — I had to help my family get used to a new environment and a new culture, but I also needed to learn how to shop and cook and speak at least the language of the marketplace.

As a diplomat's wife, I was expected to entertain, which I quickly discovered I liked very much. Part of what I saw as my job was to present our national cuisine to all the other foreign diplomats, almost for their official approval. No treaties or agreements were ever made on the basis of good food at an embassy party — or at least none that I can document — but making a good impression in this arena was terribly important to Ken's job. It was a challenge that was sometimes daunting but always exciting to me.

In addition to overseeing the work of my kitchen staff, I started trying out my skills again with French food and with Cambodian specialties, serving them to our guests from around the world. Time after time, people would say to me — it's funny, I can hear the words so clearly — "You should open up a restaurant," or "Nyep, you really must have a restaurant." It was something people said, but never anything I gave a thought to.

On April 17, 1975, Ken and I attended the funeral of Chiang Kai-shek, along with other diplomats and foreign dignitaries, at the Presidential Palace in Taipei, the capital of Taiwan, where we had been living for five years. At the reception that followed, I met Nelson Rockefeller and talked with him about the unstable political situation in Cambodia. The country was deeply embroiled in a civil war between the U.S.-backed government of Lon Nol, who had replaced King Norodom Sihanouk following a coup in 1970, and the communist insurgent revolutionaries, the Khmer Rouge, who were thought to be close to victory.

Three weeks earlier, I had flown to Phnom Penh to try to persuade members of Ken's family and my own to come to Taiwan (as my parents had done earlier that year), where they could wait out the end of the war in safety. Ken had already lost relatives in the fighting, and the capital was under intense fire the whole time I was there. I was able to get only three nephews and one of my younger sisters to leave Phnom Penh with me. My mother, who had come back to be with her mother, who was too old to travel, refused to leave.

Later in the afternoon of April 17, Ken and I listened to a radio report announcing that Cambodia had fallen to the Khmer Rouge and that the rebel troops were already marching into Phnom Penh as victors. And then there was silence. Days went by, then weeks and months, with no other official report or word of what was happening, except for the rumors and unbelievable first-person accounts of people who had somehow managed to escape: stories of savage cruelty and violence, of sanctioned executions and random murders at the hands of the Khmer Rouge. We heard of the immediate, massive evacuation of millions from the capital over the course of a single day, but we could not believe it, nor could we imagine that the stories of resettlement into forced labor camps around the countryside — part of the revolution's plan to re-turn Cambodia to a wholly peasant society — were true.

Ken was trying desperately to make contact with the new government, to get news of our families and to get permission to return home, where he hoped to offer his diplomatic skills. When we finally did get some official word, it came from the CIA, informing us that my older sister's husband, the Chief of the Cambodian Navy, was believed to have died at the hands of the Khmer Rouge on that first day of the takeover. It was assumed that my other relatives who held similar governmental positions — including my oldest brother, who had been the Minister of Commerce — had also died.

Suddenly all possibility of returning to Cambodia vanished completely, at the same time that Ken's job in Taiwan was becoming increasingly untenable — how could he be a representative if there was no country to represent? For Ken, this meant the dramatic and untimely end to his career. For the family, it meant that we were forced into exile.

In the months stretching into years that followed, we eventually found asylum in France and ended up in Béziers, a small Spanish-influenced town in the southwest, not far from the Mediterranean, where the surviving members of my family were reconvening. My two brothers-in-law and my brother were presumed dead, and there continued to be no word of my mother or grandmother, my youngest sister or any of Ken's family. Of these, only my sister survived.

As our savings dwindled and it became unmistakably clear that there would be no future diplomatic positions for Ken, we faced a financial crisis. Taking inventory of our marketable skills, I pawned some of my jewelry, and in

April 1980, we opened a restaurant called Amrita — from the Sanskrit word for "the elixir of eternal life." Without even realizing it, we now operated one of the first Cambodian restaurants in the world.

I was the chef, the girls had a number of different jobs and Ken was the maître d'. It pained me to see Ken working in this way — a man who had never even had to fill his own water glass — but this was our fate. The work was hard, the days were long, but we all survived — as did the restaurant — and even thrived. Launa and Nadsa both finished school and got jobs. Launa married a Frenchman, Gérard Lopez, who is now a chef at The Elephant Walk. And Bob Perry, Nadsa's high school sweetheart, an American whom she had met in Taiwan, came looking for her after many years, and they were eventually married.

Three years after Nadsa moved with Bob to the States, Ken and I sold the 10-year-old Amrita and moved to Boston to join them. At that point, we probably had even fewer plans for the future than we'd had when we arrived in France as refugees. But food, once again, opened a path. A year later, in August 1991, Bob and I opened The Elephant Walk restaurant in Somerville, Massachusetts, right next to Cambridge, ad-

vertising ourselves as "serving traditional Cambodian and French cuisine." It was Bob's mother who had suggested the name, the title of an old Elizabeth Taylor movie, and because of the prominence of the elephant in Khmer art and lore, it seemed a good choice.

To our delight, Americans responded enthusiastically to our food. Surprised at first by its delicacy and refinement, they soon become addicted. They seem to appreciate its healthful quality, the lightness of our salads and soups, the abundance of vegetables and fruits and the wonderful freshness of it all.

In 1994, we opened a second Elephant Walk restaurant in Boston, and in 1997, we launched Carambola in Waltham, where we serve Cambodian food only, family-style, to a packed house. Shortly thereafter, we moved our original restaurant to Cambridge and opened a small market there to make it easier for people to learn about and find the ingredients they need to make Cambodian food at home. In the midst of all of these other activities, we conceived this cookbook as another way to share what has sustained us.

The recipes in this book represent both the sophisticated foods I grew up eating at home on the most formal of occasions and at the highest levels of society and the simpler fare I routinely sampled in the marketplace and bought from vendors plying their wares along the streets of the city, the rural village and the seaside town. Whatever their source, these traditional dishes exhibit an artistry and excellence that have pleased my palate or captured my imagination in some way, and it is in this sense that I think of them as "best." Like all cooks, I've made adjustments in the recipes, sometimes without even meaning to, to suit my particular taste and circumstance, but my intention has always been to honor the traditional cuisine of my forebears.

With the fracturing of the Khmer society in recent years, like many of its cultural treasures, the finest of the traditional cuisine of Cambodia — both simple and elaborate — stands to be lost forever. Most of the people who cared deeply about food have been killed, have fled the country or have died of old age. At this point, I wouldn't know where to begin to look for the old women who used to guard the secrets of the best spice mixes for curry, preserving them for future generations to enjoy. I assume that these women are all gone.

When our family visited Cambodia recently, I was both encouraged and concerned to see a thriving restaurant community in Phnom Penh that had never existed when we last lived there. On the far side of the Japanese Friendship Bridge, which replaces an older bridge destroyed by the Khmer Rouge, we saw one new building after another standing above the lotus-covered marshes, their wraparound, Western-style decks laid out with plastic tables and chairs. In sharp contrast to the general bombed-out appearance and lack of amenities downtown, here generators hummed, radios played and Johnnie Walker signs blinked, as Cambodian food was served to a mostly tourist trade.

The food was generally good. The grilled fish with peanuts, mint, red pepper, tamarind juice and fish eggs served with raw vegetables was just as I remembered it. The spicy stir-fried chicken was hot and salty, the way it tastes best. And my first drink of green coconut juice after all these years

brought tears to my eyes. (There was another teary moment in the garden of my parents' old house, when some of the survivors of the Khmer Rouge regime who had found Phnom Penh nearly empty upon their return and claimed parts of our house as their own offered us fruit from the only tree still bearing. It was a star fruit — carambola — and we ate it together, Ken and I and our daughters and our sons-in-laws, in a silence of communion.)

But much about the food has also changed. We encountered the traditional Cambodian *Loc Lac* (Marinated Beef with Lime Sauce) being served with french fries in one place and with fried eggs in the next, a telltale sign of the recent presence of Western patrons (there were, after all, some 20,000 U.N. personnel assigned to Cambodia in the early nineties to set up national elections). The flavors overall struck me as harsh — most often too much lemongrass and too much sugar — which I assume is the result of so many Cambodians having lived in refugee camps in Thailand. The more complicated the dish, the less successful the results, and I found myself missing the subtlety of the cooking I had grown up with.

This experience gave me even greater resolve to commit to paper the recipes for traditional Cambodian dishes, which I consider a valuable cultural inheritance. With this book, I hope not only to share some of Cambodia's riches with a Western audience, but also to refresh the memories of some

of my own countrymen, perhaps expanding their knowledge at the same time. For unless some of the traditional ways are revived now, the next generation won't have anything to remember.

The responsibility involved in writing the first Cambodian cookbook has felt daunting at times. I have worried that other Cambodians might feel that I've omitted the best dishes or included ones they've never heard of, or — probably the most likely — that the way I make a dish is wrong (which means different from the way they make it). I think I have resigned myself to the likelihood of all of these responses, as I suspect I would feel the same reading someone else's book about *my* food.

To friends, strangers and critics alike, I would like to say that my highest aim in writing this book has always been to honor my country, my people, my mother — and the many mothers who did not live to share their great culinary skills and knowledge with their children — as well as the food itself. I offer it to all of you just as it has always been offered to me, as a gift.

THE RICH HISTORY OF CAMBODIAN CUISINE

To most Americans, Cambodia, if it conjures up anything at all, tends to trigger lingering images of wartime atrocities from the movie *The Killing Fields* or vague impressions of more recent political unrest from the nightly news. People in the West simply don't know very much about the history and culture of Cambodia, so it is no surprise they don't know anything about the food.

To the outsider, Cambodia may appear to be an exotic land, full of mystery, paradox and perplexity. The intense spirituality of the place and its natural rawness, its great riches and deprivations, the climatic extremes and the gentleness of the Cambodian people, standing in sharp contrast with the recent period of genocide under the Khmer Rouge, both challenge and confound the mind. In this context, one of the flavor combinations that Cambodians value so much, sweet and sour — and, even more pointedly, sweet and bitter — take on a much broader meaning.

Cambodia's history reminds me of one of the exquisite silks produced by our artisans: a rich interweaving of many cultural influences that begins in prehistory with the contributions of India and Java, includes the interactions of the regional ethnic kingdoms, and results, in the ninth century, with the emergence of an indigenous Cambodian, or Khmer, culture. The ongoing impact of China and intense struggles over many centuries with our neighbors — Thai, Vietnamese and Lao — have all left their mark on our culture. The influence of the West was first felt at the end of the sixteenth century, when Portuguese and Spanish missionaries and opportunists arrived, followed shortly thereafter by Dutch traders, and, in the eighteenth century, by the French, who came, conquered and stayed to rule Cambodia as a protectorate for nearly a hundred years.

Nestled in the center of Southeast Asia, or Indochina, as the region has also been called in recognition of the two powerful nations that surround it, Cambodia is the smallest country in the region in square miles, only about the size of Washington State. According to the earliest known records, the area of present-day Cambodia was ruled for the first four centuries A.D. by the Indianized state known only by its Chinese name, Funan. It was later succeeded by one of its vassal states, the kingdom of Chen-la, which expanded and consolidated its regional holdings into a strong and stable confederacy over the next several centuries.

INDIAN INFLUENCES, NEIGHBORING THREATS

During this time, trade with India and Indianized Java had an enormous impact on the culture of the Khmer people, the ancestors of today's Cambodians. Skirts inspired by the Indian sari were worn by Khmer men and women, along with the traditional turban, the *krama*. The Hindu and Buddhist religions, medieval Indian architectural style and the Pali-like Khmer script are also legacies of this Indianizing process. So, too, is the significant part of the Cambodian cuisine that is curry-based and the custom of eating everything but noodle dishes with a spoon instead of chopsticks.

In the ninth century, a Khmer Empire of Angkor emerged. It went on to hold sway in the region for more than six centuries. Its power was based in large part on a successful system of irrigation and reservoirs that allowed for a significant increase in rice production, which in turn supported ever-larger populations. At the height of Angkorian rule during the eleventh and twelfth centuries, the empire supported some 30 million people, and its capital city, Angkor, which had previously been barren land, had a population of more than one million.

Bolstered by sophisticated engineering and effective political structures, Cambodia's "classical period" produced magnificent works of art and architecture in sandstone and laterite. Angkor's central temple, Angkor Wat, which was first dedicated to the Hindu god, Vishnu, and later to Buddha, is the largest single religious structure in the world, using almost as much stone as the Great Pyramid. The Angkor Empire also produced an elaborate form of classical court dance and music and a sophisticated, refined cuisine that impressed itself on the entire region.

During the fifteenth century, the power of the Angkor

Empire began to erode, as the neighboring Thai, Vietnamese and Lao kingdoms, which had formerly been subsumed under it, grew stronger and more aggressive. With each new attack from the outside, the rich lands of the once great empire were divided and annexed. Some believe, in fact, that had the French not claimed Cambodia as a protectorate in 1863, the country would eventually have been completely absorbed by Vietnam and Thailand. The greatest achievements of the Angkor Empire, honed by centuries of imperial status and advanced civilization, all but disappeared from view — literally swallowed up by the jungle — only to be "discovered" by French archaeologists in the mid-nineteenth century.

"YEAR ZERO": THE CIVIL WAR

Following a brief period of occupation by the Japanese during World War II, Cambodia finally wrested full independence from the French in 1953 under the leadership of its king, Norodom Sihanouk. He later abdicated the throne in order to be elected chief of state in 1955 and changed his title to prince. In 1970, he was ousted by an American-backed coup because he allegedly gave aid to communist North Vietnam, despite Cambodia's declaration of neutrality.

A civil war ensued between the U.S.-supported government under Lon Nol and followers of the ousted Sihanouk. Sihanouk's supporters were largely composed of an underground communist movement known as the Khmer Rouge ("red Cambodians"), a nationalistic group that wanted to rid the country of foreign imperialists, abolish class divisions and return Cambodia to an indigenous peasant culture. The extensive and illegal American bombings of Cambodia in 1973, designed to attack the Vietcong, who were moving supplies through Cambodia, only helped to fuel the growing peasant-based resistance to foreign intervention, and, in April 1975, the communist rebels finally took the country. Under Pol Pot and a cadre of close advisers, the new revolutionary government set about to create overnight a quasi–Marxist-Leninist peasant society by returning Cambodia to what they called Year Zero: a society, as one historian characterized it, without "money, markets, formal education, Buddhism, books, private property . . . and freedom of movement" and — needless to say — without cuisine.

The impact of this era, the time of "the killing fields," can hardly be overstated.

Less than four years later, in 1979, the Khmer Rouge were driven out by Vietnamese forces in retaliation for their attack on Vietnam, but their policies and practices had resulted in the deaths of more than a million Cambodians from starvation, overwork, disease or torture. Decades later, the country still struggles to rebuild.

After 10 years of "protecting" Cambodia, under continuous criticism from the international community, the Vietnamese withdrew from the country in 1989. In 1992, the United Nations sent international peacekeepers to oversee the repatriation of the more than 300,000 Cambodians who had fled to Thai refugee camps and to set up and monitor free elections. The uneasy coalition that resulted between the Sihanouk royalists and the followers of the Vietnamese-backed government broke down in 1997, and politics in Cambodia have remained uncertain ever since. The predicted demise of the Khmer Rouge following the death of Pol Pot in April 1998 is far from realized, as the divisions between rich and poor and between city and country that fostered the civil war in the first place continue to exist.

A WILD LAND OF RICH RESOURCES

While the culture of Cambodia exhibits great refinement and subtlety, it is also still wild. I have never seen a better illustration than the temple ruins at Angkor, where the sinuous roots of giant fig and kapok trees cradle the magnificent man-made structures built to honor the gods, at the same time that they break them apart. The carved celestial dancers, the *apsaras*, dance delicately along the temple walls in direct counterpoint to the ravaging energies of the surrounding jungles, the land mines they contain and the broader ferocity of Cambodia's recent past.

Cambodia has been shaped not only by international influences and complicated politics, but also by a fascinating mixture of physical elements. A "Great Lake," the Tonle Sap, lies at the country's center. Fed and drained by the Tonle Sap River and the Mekong River, which have for centuries provided most of the travel and communication routes for the country, as well as its food supply, the lake more than triples in size during the rainy season, making it the largest reserve of freshwater fish in the world. Its great wealth of plant and animal life is mined by the

thousands of fishermen who live in houseboats along its shores.

At the end of the rainy season, in late November, when the waters of the lake crest and begin to run backward, fishermen throw out nets for the millions of freshwater fish being sent down the Mekong River toward the sea. When this amazing run of fish comes to an end, *prahok* season begins and the whole of Cambodia becomes caught up with its preparation.

To make the *prahok*, or preserved fish, Cambodians pound the fish until the skins break, rub them with coarse rock salt and lay them out to dry for a day or two, until the juices of the fish stop dripping. Then they pack the fish into large bamboo baskets and take them to the river, where they submerge the baskets in flowing water to clean the fish. They pound the fish again, this time with their feet (as grapes are mashed for wine), and remove the bones, scales and entrails. Now in small pieces, the fish is resalted, packed into large ceramic jars and set aside for three or four more months to "ripen." When I was growing up, my mother would always be busy at this time of year, working with the servants to prepare the vast quantities of fish. All you could hear, day and night, was the chop, chop, chopping, and all you could smell was fish.

Surrounding Cambodia's Great Lake, the low-lying plains make up the largest part of the country. The plains are brown for half the year, but after the rainy season replenishes their fertile soil with its annual flooding, they become a patchwork of lush green rice paddies. For this reason, the lowlands are called "the rice bowl." They are ringed on three sides by highlands, dense jungles and heavily forested mountains, which provide natural boundaries to the south and east with Vietnam and to the north with Laos and Thailand. In the southwest, the mountains give way on the seaward side to virgin rain forest and then to a narrow but beautiful strip of beach along the Gulf of Siam.

THE BUSTLING CENTER: PHNOM PENH

In contrast to this undeveloped countryside is the capital city, where all of the country's rich resources converge. Transport yourself there and you'll see its streets filled with bicycle-driven rickshaws, or *cyclos*, with their passenger seats piled high with produce bound for market: woven bamboo trays filled with crimson lychee fruit and knobby brown tamarind pods, branches of dark green kaffir lime leaves, large boxes of eggs. Small motorbikes, called *motos*, whiz by with other cargo: a freshly slaughtered pig, crates of bananas and huge sacks of rice. Alongside the busy thoroughfares, people sit or squat by small stands and tiny hole-in-the-wall eateries, watching the parade of comestibles passing by as they jab with chopsticks into their bowls of broth, slurping up noodles and pieces of fried garlic, bright red chilies and some fish or bits of meat.

Young Buddhist monks in saffron-colored robes make their early morning rounds, alms bowls in hand, to beg for their daily sustenance. The sounds of chanting and prayer fill the city's temples and *wats*, the monasteries, where senior monks sit surrounded by lotus flowers and wrapped in the smoke of burning incense to receive offerings of cigarettes, fruit, garlands of jasmine flowers and stacks of silver serving dishes filled with food, all given by the faithful in hopes of securing merit for themselves and their ancestors. As the sun reaches the midheaven, the monks turn their thoughts from food toward study and prayer, beginning their daily fast until the following dawn.

Outside the monastery walls, the traffic continues to move briskly through the city streets. A man riding behind an oversized ice chest, on top of which he has balanced colorful bottles of mango, orange and papaya juice, pedals along next to a chauffeur-driven Mercedes-Benz. Women easing their shiny metal carts stacked high with freshly baked baguettes into the flow of traffic head out to other dusty thoroughfares around the city to park and set up shop. At the far side of the road, but still within its current, an old man in a sarong, the native skirt, carries large baskets full of peanuts that hang from either end of the bamboo pole slung across his shoulders, one in front, one behind.

At Phnom Penh's *Psaar T'mei*, the Central Market, everything from household goods to hardware to clothing to food is offered for sale. East and West meet: brass coins used for drawing "bad blood" from a sick body sit alongside fax machines and modems; plastics are placed next to bamboo and palm products. At the market's center, where children beg for money, you'll find some of the country's finest craft works: elegant silver pieces and gold jewelry set with rubies and sapphires from the Pailin Hills to the west, resplendent silks from the Muslim Cham weavers of Takeo to the south and Kampong Cham Province to the northeast. Beggars approaching the early arrivals motion toward their mouths with the fin-

gertips of one hand held together, repeating, "*N'yam, n'yam*" — part question, part order — "Eat? Eat!"

One whole side of the market is filled with things to eat. There are vegetables and fruit of every imagining and provenance, displays of herbs and spices in red plastic bowls, neon-colored jellied sweets, skeins of translucent bean thread noodles and bag after bag filled with rice, rice flours and rice noodles. Next to racks of squawking chickens hang pieces of meat, sausages, organs and entrails. Huge ceramic jars filled with fermenting fish are flanked by bottles of fish sauce and stacks of salted fish tied together like shiny surprise gift packages; next to them stand tables piled high with just-caught fish, still wriggling, and baskets of bright blue freshwater lobsters, their spindly front claws outstretched. Above them, festoons of dried squid hang like miniature kites.

Down every aisle, vendors busily grind coconut meat, weigh out rice flour, rock babies, gut fish, simmer curries, soak noodles and stir thick palm sugar syrups. There is always something to eat and always someone — usually a lot of someones — eating.

Across the street from the market, food carts and stands cater to shoppers. One woman behind a glass-fronted cart fills a baguette with different kinds of pâté and pickled vegetables and folds salt and pepper and tiny red chilies neatly into little green paper packets. In one of the parks, a vendor standing behind a makeshift table deftly slices away the top of a green coconut, slides a couple of straws into it and offers up the delicately sweet fresh juice to people strolling by. The cooler at her feet is most likely filled with aluminum cans of soy milk, winter melon tea, grass jelly tea and a concoction called *grob chi,* a clotted white liquid made with basil seeds.

At this point, a small boy approaches, holding up a crudely made wooden cage filled with tiny finches. His bare legs and feet, his face, his ragged shirt and his torn oversized pants cinched with a piece of rope at the waist are the color of the dusty earth. His eyes are dark and wide. "Buy a bird," he begs, "and make a wish — anything you want. Then let the prayers fly up to heaven."

THE FOOD OF CAMBODIA

Americans visiting Cambodia are often struck by the prominence of food in daily life. Everywhere and at all hours, they see people visibly engaged with food: growing, picking, carrying, cooking, buying, selling and eating. From a morning bowl of noodle soup in Siem Reap near the great temples of Angkor to a midday meal of crab and prawns along the Tonle Sap Lake or a plate of curried deer meat in the shadow of the Dangrek Mountains in the north, food is central to the sense of identity. From the fanciest French meal at one of the restaurants in Phnom Penh to the alfresco dinners of the homeless families now living in the city's parks, Cambodians affirm that eating is not only a physical necessity, but also an act of cultural importance.

From its many natural and cultural resources, Cambodian cuisine draws the inspiration and materials to produce a lively, varied fare. From India, by way of Java, we inherited the art of blending spice pastes for stews and curries, using cardamom, ginger, cinnamon, star anise, tamarind, turmeric and cilantro, to which we added garlic and shallots and the indigenous lemongrass, galangal and its close relative the rhizome and citrus-flavored kaffir lime leaves. The Chinese introduced us to soy sauce and noodles, a host of new

vegetables, the arts of stir-frying and steaming and the custom of having soup for the morning meal. The Portuguese and Spanish brought chili peppers, beans, tomatoes and corn. The French contributed valuable culinary techniques, such as baking, and fabulous bread.

For those who are familiar with the foods from our neighboring region, Cambodian cuisine is less sweet than Thai food, less salty than Vietnamese and subtler overall. We appreciate sweetness in the form of palm and cane sugar, and we especially like it in desserts mixed with thick, rich coconut milk. We are particularly fond of saltiness, even in our fruits, and use lots of fish sauce, just as the Chinese rely on soy sauce, to add this quality. Sour is another popular taste, which we get from tamarind, lime juice, unripe fruits and pickles. We use vegetables like the pea eggplant and bitter melon for our bitter component and add fiery hot chilies to make all of the other flavors come to life.

Because of the abundance and variety of fruits and vegetables, we serve them fresh at every meal, in almost everything we eat. The fact that we don't make a big distinction between fruits and vegetables allows us enormous flexibility in this regard. Our routine herb choices — lemongrass, kaffir lime, ginger and garlic, for example — are especially aromatic. As in Chinese cuisine, there is also a keen sensory appreciation for textures, and we like to vary them in interesting ways, for instance, by topping a stew with crisply fried shallots or adding crunchy, succulent bean sprouts to a dish of slippery noodles. We have very definite standards for how the food should look, not only that garnishes should be clever and colorful, but that sauces should have a certain dark shade and curries the right oily sheen.

The staple of the Cambodian diet is rice, just as it is throughout the rest of Southeast Asia, and even the poorest peasant will always have some on hand. As the sine qua non of every meal, rice accompanies and, to some extent, interprets all the rest of what is eaten. What Westerners would consider soups, we treat more as richly flavored, embellished broths meant for spooning over rice or eating with rice noodles; the same is true for our many braises and stews. Cambodian stir-fries, quick and economical to make, are transformed into balanced and filling meals when eaten with rice.

After rice, fish is the most common feature of the Cambodian diet. Except for people who live along the coast and the ethnic Chinese, Cambodians tend to prefer the freshwater fish so abundant in the Tonle Sap Lake, and they incorporate it into every aspect of their diet. Salads of salted crab and papaya served with mint and tomatoes sit on the table next to lime-cured white fish mixed with vegetables and soup made of banana blossom and eel. Perhaps the most popular way to prepare fresh fish is to grill it, with nothing more than green mango and fish sauce on the side. A more elaborate meal would include a variety of other ingredients and seasonings.

Fish also appears deep-fried, stir-fried, seared, steamed, braised and curried, and in every imaginable combination. Freshwater lobster is particularly valued for its delicate sweetness, and it transforms any dish in which it appears into something special — from a simple stir-fry with salted daikon to an imperial offering made with coconut milk and sticky rice. Cambodians also greatly enjoy the delicacy of the tiny freshwater clams, whether salted and sun-dried, sautéed with basil or served with a coconut milk and spice sauce.

Just as important as fresh fish is the whole range of preserved fish — dried, salted, smoked and fermented — that makes its way to the table. Two of its most common forms are fish sauce and the fermented fish paste, *prahok*, which are made by a process of preserving and are nothing short of defining flavors for Khmer cuisine. While fish sauce seems to be served in and with just about everything, *prahok* is used with greater reserve, so that when it does appear, it signals the food as distinctly Cambodian. To me, it makes the dish taste like home.

Along the coast, recipes that celebrate saltwater fish are more common, and some have become inextricably linked with the places in which they arose, as in the case of the Deep-Fried Pomfret prepared with garlic, sugar, lime juice and chilies, for which the town of Kampot used to be renowned. In Kep, which was founded as a colonial resort on the Gulf of Siam in 1917 and totally destroyed by the Khmer Rouge in the 1970s, restaurants once stood beside a beautiful promenade, offering elegant seafood dishes to an elite clientele. Today, individual vendors line up along the beach to serve simpler fare: crabs sautéed with onions and lots of black pepper, or pieces of dried squid, pounded and grilled over a wood fire, accompanied by pickled green papaya and cucumbers.

In the northern part of the country, along the border, the Thai influence is evident in the increased amount of coconut milk. Flavors are stronger there — dishes are sweeter and hotter — and the forests provide deer, wild birds and other game for the table. Bamboo shoots, the mainstay of the Lao diet, appear more frequently in a variety of dishes. Spice pastes of red and green are also common. In the northwest, in the shadow of Angkor, an ancient imperial gastronomy can be glimpsed in complex dishes like *amok*, a wonderful combination of fish, coconut milk and a blending of seasonings traditionally presented in an ingenious container made of banana leaves.

More pronounced than any regional distinctions is the difference between Cambodia's rural and urban cuisines. The diet of the country's peasants tends to be simple, largely dependent on what the people can grow and procure themselves. Their markets are few and sparsely stocked, and their resources to buy goods are limited, in any case. Beef is rare, and although people in the country commonly raise pigs and chickens, the meat is nonetheless used sparingly. Because spices are often hard to get, they tend to be costly; for that reason, and because of the time required to hand-grate the meat and press the milk from coconuts, the rural people tend to make few curry dishes, only for special rituals and holidays.

In the cities, where markets are well stocked and plentiful and the economies more expansive, the cuisine is noticeably more developed, with a wider variety, though there are still marked differences between the eating habits of the rich and the poor. Several of the recipes in this book, such as Five-Spice Chicken with Dates (page 188), Royal Catfish Enrobed with Coconut Milk and Lemongrass (page 163), Pork with Peanuts and Lilies (page 139) and Golden Angel Hair (page 280), are representative of *haute cuisine,* often having originated in the imperial court. With the ready availability in the United States of such prepared food items as coconut milk, fish paste, tamarind juice concentrate and canned fruits and vegetables, the American cook can prepare even the fanciest of these dishes with relative ease.

Other dishes represent the simpler fare: grilled chicken and fish, vegetable relishes, perfectly composed stir-fries. Like their more elaborate counterparts, they also reflect a process of honing and refinement over time. All you need to do is taste *Nataing* (page 52), the fabulous dish made of ground pork and thinly sliced garlic mixed with roasted peanuts and coconut milk and flavored with ground chilies, to appreciate the process.

The best of all traditional Cambodian cuisine, whether rural or urban, simple or elaborate, is characterized by extra attention to detail and delicacy. Its spirit has little to do with wealth and fuss and everything to do with connoisseurship. The freshest ingredients, the brightest flavors and an inviting appearance: these are my mantras, and they are goals that anyone can attain.

SHOPPING FOR CAMBODIAN INGREDIENTS

For much of the cooking in this book, you don't have to travel any farther than your neighborhood food store. Mainstream supermarkets increasingly cater to ethnic customers and are expanding their stock accordingly, particularly in the produce section. Items like daikon, ginger, coconuts and mung bean sprouts have become almost commonplace. Where there once were only two or three varieties of rice to choose from, there are now often six or seven, including, if not the Cambodian favorite, jasmine rice, then a flavorful substitute like basmati. Chili peppers and herbs now proliferate. Ingredients once considered exotic, like tofu, mustard greens, raw peanuts, fresh basil, dried mushrooms, English cucumbers and papayas are now relatively easy to find. On occasion, I've seen even lemongrass with the produce in one of my local supermarkets, freshwater lobster with the seafood, and fish sauce and tamarind with the Asian products.

Naturally, some ingredients central to Cambodian cuisine aren't available in Western grocery stores, and the more authentic you want your food to taste, the more adventuresome you'll become. Most of the preserved fish products, for example—shrimp paste, dried shrimp, fish powder and the fermented *prahok*—have to be purchased at Asian markets or through mail-order suppliers (a list of sources begins on page 309). Other signature flavors like kaffir lime leaves and galangal, which have no adequate substitutes, are also available in Asian markets. I have tried to make the process of finding these foods easier by including photographs in the Glossary.

Most large cities in this country, and even some of the small ones, have a Chinatown, or at least a Chinese market, which will carry the great majority of items on your shopping list. Specifically Southeast Asian markets have also sprung up across the country wherever substantial numbers of these immigrant populations are living (the largest concentrations of Cambodians are currently in the Long Beach area in California and the Greater Boston area). In these stores, you will find everything you need—and then some.

A few core ingredients bought in quantities sufficient for stockpiling can stand you in good stead for a long time. I always buy multiple packets of bean thread noodles, 25-pound bags of rice and several cans of coconut milk in a trip. Lemongrass and kaffir lime leaves freeze very well, which means you can store vast quantities without sacrificing quality. Ingredients like frozen banana leaves and spring roll wrappers take up very little storage space but allow you—or even inspire you—to make great impromptu dishes. I usually start planning a meal based on what I see at the store and then fill in with whatever I have on hand at home; once your Cambodian larder is in place, you will be able to do the same thing. You can count on most of the prepared foods—dried, bottled, canned and frozen—to store well, and even the infrequently used items, such as dried lilies, lotus seeds, red dates and a jar of rhizomes, seem to last forever.

In the summer, I have also had great luck growing my own produce. Lemongrass is easy to root in water, and I keep a big pot of it on my back porch, where I grow a number of other plants for cooking. Asian herbs and "Thai peppers" (bird's eye chilies) show up frequently in garden centers and catalogs, and in Chinatown you can find seed packets for plants like Chinese watercress, Chinese celery and bitter melon.

Shopping in an Asian market can be an exhilarating, challenging and sometimes confusing experience, but one that I highly recommend. In part, it gives you a head start at understanding what you're going to prepare and eat. It is likely that you will encounter a different worldview from your own, one that affects what counts as food, how it is presented and even how the store is organized.

If the thought of weaving your way through six-foot-high stalks of sugarcane or large, spiky durian fruit, with its infamous strong odor, past duck tongues, frog legs and bean curd molded to look like giant scaled fish, tickles your fancy, then you'll love shopping in an Asian market. The carnival aspect will enthrall you, and I suspect you will try to infuse the foods you cook with some of this same excitement. (If you think these stores are wild and wonderful, you would probably love the open-air markets of Asia, where the encounter with your next meal is even more direct and intimate.)

You will need to have a certain level of tolerance for "translation" issues. Signs will routinely be written in a language you don't know or in an English that doesn't make sense to you. Or the English will make sense but won't be accurate: for example, the Chinese often refer to daikon as both a radish, which it is, and a turnip, which it is not. Pickled leek bulbs will be called "pickled scallions." And some—though not all—of the jars of *pra-hok* (fermented fish solids) will have labels claiming they are "fish sauce."

But don't worry: the Glossary will help you find the ingredients you need, and after a trip or two to the market and a little time in the kitchen, you'll feel like an honorary Cambodian. The end result of these culinary excursions will be not only a lot of good eating, but also a broader horizon. There's a good chance that you will be exhilarated when you see how baby bananas grow inside a blossom or discover the taste of green coconut juice (one of my greatest pleasures) or bite into a soft cake made of rice flour for the first time. Eating fruits green, roasting and grinding rice, tasting different kinds of chilies—there's so much to try and so much to enjoy. If all you do is come away with a new brand of chili sauce, an appreciation for freshwater fish and a growing taste for noodle soup at odd hours of the day, I will be very pleased.

For information on
individual ingredients, see the
Glossary beginning on page 283.

NOTES ON SERVING

The Cambodian way is to put all the food out on the table at the same time. There is no hierarchy that governs which dish is eaten first or considered the centerpiece. Soups don't get eaten before the meal, salads don't get eaten after and meat isn't the main course. Needless to say, there's nothing to stop you from serving these Cambodian dishes American-style in courses or from introducing them individually into an otherwise Western meal.

In addition to the various bowls and platters, Cambodians set out small bowls of fish sauce, soy sauce, salt and pepper, kaffir lime slices and sliced red bird's eye chilies. Jasmine tea, cold water and fresh rice are constantly offered and replenished (I find that fresh fruit juices, good beer and chilled rosé also make good beverage options). Forks and spoons are put out on the table, and chopsticks if noodles are going to be served.

The Cambodian style of eating is quite different from the American one. Holding the spoon in the right hand and the fork in the left, a Cambodian diner uses the fork to fill up the spoon, first with some rice and then with some of the stew or stir-fry—whatever dish is being sampled at the moment. Some herbs or relish, a squeeze of kaffir lime juice, and a few slices of chilies and fish sauce will be added so that each bite is prepared exactly to taste. If you have never eaten this way before, I heartily recommend it—it's not only great fun, but also very satisfying.

In Cambodia, the number of dishes at a given meal will depend in part on the occasion and also on how well-off the family is. In providing yields for the recipes in this book, I have tried to take cultural differences into account and have generally assumed that the American public is likely to serve a single main course. Should you decide to prepare more than one of these dishes for one meal, keep in mind that you will probably be able to feed many more people than the four servings indicated.

APPETIZERS AND SNACKS

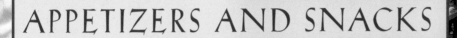

IN TRADITIONAL KHMER CULTURE, THERE IS NO SUCH culinary category as appetizer because the whole meal is served buffet-style. This notion of having something to eat before the meal came to Cambodia in fairly recent history by way of the French, and it was my father who introduced it into our family. When I was growing up, he would often invite his French colleagues to the house for drinks and something to eat, most of which would be traditional entrees that my mother had adapted to this new concept of entertaining. All my brothers and sisters looked forward to having company, and I used to love to pass the food around to our guests.

If appetizers are not a Khmer concept, then snacking certainly is. Because our lives are very active, the climate is extremely hot, and our meals are generally light, we tend to eat frequently — some even say constantly — throughout the day. That's one of the reasons there is so much street food available, so we can grab something to eat wherever we are and no matter what else we're doing.

In this chapter, I have included recipes for some of my favorite Cambodian street foods — Grilled Corn and Spicy Chicken Wings, for example — which are terrific all by themselves, but which you can easily incorporate into a meal as well. Some of the other recipes, like the broiled clams and the brochettes, which were adapted from Khmer dishes in the first place, can be transformed back to main courses without effort. Then there are Shrimp Toasts, two kinds of spring rolls and Red Pork with Coconut Milk, which you can serve over Crispy Rice or French bread. All are so delicious that they transcend categories and courses altogether — I say eat them whenever, with whatever you like.

SHRIMP TOASTS
Nom Pang Chien B'kong

MAKES 20 TO 25 TOASTS

1 pound shrimp, shelled and deveined

6 garlic cloves, coarsely chopped

1 medium shallot, coarsely chopped

2½ tablespoons water

1 tablespoon sugar

½ teaspoon salt

¼ teaspoon freshly ground pepper

2 scallions, sliced ¼ inch thick

1 medium baguette, cut into 20–25 slices, each
    slightly less than ½ inch thick

2 cups vegetable oil

Asian chili sauce

The combination of deep-fried sweet shrimp with garlic and shallot has proved nearly irresistible to diners at The Elephant Walk. Delicious as it is, however, this appetizer is very simple to make. A French baguette is perfect for this recipe, but any other good bread — except for something with a strong taste like sourdough, which would overpower the shrimp — will also work well.

Blend the shrimp, garlic, shallot, water, sugar, salt and pepper together in a blender or food processor until smooth, 1½ to 2 minutes. Transfer to a bowl and combine with the scallions.

Spread about 1 tablespoon of the shrimp mixture on each slice of bread, mounding it slightly in the center; the mixture will adhere to the bread.

Heat the oil in a large pot or deep-fryer over medium-high heat to 350°F (a cube of bread tossed in will sizzle and quickly brown). Fry the toasts in batches until golden brown all over, about a minute per side. Remove with a slotted spoon and drain on paper towels. Serve immediately with chili sauce.

CRISPY PORK TOASTS WITH SCALLIONS
Nom Pang Chien Saik Chrouk

MAKES 20 TO 25 TOASTS

1 pound ground pork
8 garlic cloves, coarsely chopped
1 medium shallot, coarsely chopped
1½ tablespoons water
1 tablespoon sugar
½ teaspoon cornstarch or all-purpose flour
1 teaspoon salt
½ teaspoon freshly ground pepper
2 scallions, sliced ¼ inch thick
1 medium baguette, cut into 20–25 slices, each
    slightly less than ½ inch thick
2 cups vegetable oil
Asian chili sauce

In Cambodia, these deep-fried toasts are even more popular than their shrimp counterparts. They are more filling than the shrimp, and I find that two per person is usually plenty, although when I serve these at a stand-up affair, I tend to cut the toasts in half to make them easier to eat. Be sure that you serve Asian-style chili sauce, which has more garlic and sweetness than Hispanic brands and complements the pork perfectly.

Blend the pork, garlic, shallot, water, sugar, cornstarch or flour, salt and pepper together in a blender or food processor until smooth, 1½ to 2 minutes. Transfer to a bowl and combine with the scallions.

Spread about 1 tablespoon of the pork mixture on each slice of bread, mounding it slightly in the center; the mixture will adhere to the bread.

Heat the oil in a large pot or deep-fryer over medium-high heat to 350°F (a cube of bread tossed in will sizzle and quickly brown). Fry the toasts in batches until golden brown all over, about a minute per side. Remove with a slotted spoon and drain on paper towels. Serve immediately with chili sauce.

GINGER PORK WITH PEANUTS
Meang Lao

SERVES 6 TO 8

2 tablespoons vegetable oil

5 large garlic cloves, thinly sliced

4 large shallots, thinly sliced

½ pound ground pork

3 tablespoons tamarind juice

6 tablespoons sugar

1½ teaspoons salt

3 tablespoons peeled, finely chopped ginger

½ cup peanuts, roasted and coarsely ground

1 bunch (40–50 leaves) Chinese spinach or other
    smooth, flat-leaved spinach (optional)

Cilantro sprigs and sliced red bell pepper, for
    garnish (if not using the spinach)

Crispy Rice (page 203)

Heat the oil in a large skillet over medium-high heat and fry the garlic and shallots until crisp and brown but not burned, about 30 seconds. Remove with a slotted spoon and set aside.

In the same pan, brown the pork, breaking it apart as it cooks, about 3 minutes. Stir in the tamarind juice, sugar and salt. Stir in the fried garlic and shallots and the ginger. Lower the heat to medium and cook for 3 minutes more, or until the liquid has almost evaporated. Stir in the peanuts. Remove from the heat and set aside.

If you want to make little packets, dip the spinach leaves in boiling water to blanch and lay out on a towel to drain. Place a teaspoonful of the pork mixture in the center of each leaf, and fold over both sides of the leaf and then fold the top

The combination of ground pork with ginger, garlic and roasted peanuts is so enchanting that you may find yourself inviting guests over just to have an excuse to make it. The filling is usually served in Cambodia in small packets wrapped in yuca leaves, but I've found that blanched spinach works just as well. Because the accompanying Crispy Rice requires some advance preparation, I sometimes simplify this recipe by skipping the wrapping part altogether and serving the pork mixture directly from a bowl, but then I always make a nice garnish for it with sprigs of cilantro and thin slices of red bell peppers. (See the photograph on page 45.)

and bottom over. Arrange seam side down on a platter. If you decide to forgo the packets, put the pork mixture in a serving bowl and garnish with cilantro and red peppers. Serve warm or at room temperature with Crispy Rice.

CAMBODIAN SPRING ROLLS
Khmer Rouleaux

MAKES 45 TO 50 SPRING ROLLS

These spring rolls were originally Vietnamese, but they have won great favor with Cambodians, who now eat them all the time for snacks. In Cambodia, you can find *rouleaux* at food stands and restaurants, and there are even vendors who walk the city streets with all the fixings in two baskets — a tiny charcoal burner, a wok, the meat, noodles and vegetables — ready to lay everything out at your feet while they prepare this treat. Once you master the wrapping technique, this recipe is remarkably simple to make, and the crisply fried spring rolls, garnished with fresh herbs and vegetables, rolled up in a lettuce leaf and dipped in a sprightly sauce, are always a big hit.

1 small package bean thread noodles (1¾ ounces), soaked in warm water for 10–15 minutes and drained

2 cups grated carrots

1 pound ground pork

½ cup very finely chopped onions

¾ cup peanuts, roasted and coarsely ground

2 tablespoons sugar

½ teaspoon salt

¼ cup cold water

2 tablespoons all-purpose flour

2 heads green or red leaf lettuce, separated into leaves, washed and patted dry

1 cucumber, peeled and sliced ⅛ inch thick

2 cups mung bean sprouts

1 cup loosely packed fresh basil leaves

1 cup loosely packed fresh mint leaves

Dipping Sauce for Spring Rolls (page 49)

1–2 packages rice paper spring roll wrappers (preferably triangular, 6 inches to a side)

4 or more cups vegetable oil

Cut the soaked bean thread noodles into ½-inch lengths. Squeeze the grated carrots in cheesecloth or a kitchen towel to extract as much moisture as possible.

In a large bowl, combine the bean thread noodles, carrots, pork, onions, ½ cup of the peanuts, sugar and salt, blending thoroughly.

To make a paste for sealing the spring rolls, in a small saucepan, slowly add the water to the flour, stirring continuously to avoid lumps. Cook over medium-high heat, stirring, until thickened, about 2 minutes. Remove from the heat and allow to cool.

Meanwhile, arrange mounds of the lettuce, cucumber, bean sprouts, basil and mint on a platter, leaving space in the middle for the spring rolls. Prepare the dipping sauce and put in a separate bowl.

Lay out a kitchen towel on a work surface. Dip several wrappers in a shallow bowl of warm water and lay them out on the towel to soften, 1 to 2 minutes. Moisten more wrappers as needed as you prepare the spring rolls.

Place one of the wrappers with a tip pointing away from you. Using a tablespoon of the pork mixture, make a small sausage link about 3 inches long and ¾ inch thick and lay it out across the middle of the wrapper (figure 1). Fold the right and left sides of the wrapper toward the center (figure 2). Fold the bottom of the wrapper over the pork roll and roll up (figure 3). Spread a small amount of the flour-and-water paste on the tip of the wrapper (figure 4) and continue rolling; press to seal.

If you find you have difficulty keeping the wrappers from tearing, try using two wrappers per spring roll, placing the second wrapper on top of the first but about an inch lower. (You will need the second package of wrappers if you do it this way.) Whichever technique you employ, continue to

FIGURE 1

FIGURE 2

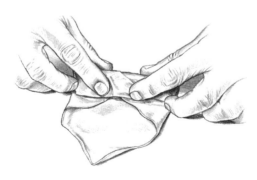

FIGURE 3

FIGURE 4

make the spring rolls until you have used up all the filling; you should be able to make 45 to 50. Leftover wrappers can be tightly wrapped and stored for later use.

Heat the oil in a large pot or deep-fryer over medium-high heat to 350°F; a cube of bread tossed in will sizzle and quickly brown. (The temperature is important: if the oil is too hot, the wrapper will cook before the filling is done; if it is not hot enough, the rolls will absorb the oil and become greasy.) Add about 10 spring rolls at a time and cook, stirring occasionally, until golden brown, 4 to 5 minutes. Remove the spring rolls with a slotted spoon from the oil as they are done and drain on paper towels. Arrange on the platter with the vegetables, sprinkle with the remaining ¼ cup peanuts and serve hot.

To eat, lay out a large lettuce leaf on your plate and put some of the cucumbers, bean sprouts, basil and mint leaves in the center, with a spring roll on top. Fold the lettuce leaf around these contents and dip in the sauce.

DIPPING SAUCE FOR SPRING ROLLS
Tuk Trey

MAKES ABOUT 1½ CUPS

¾ cup water

¾ cup sugar

⅓ cup fish sauce

¼ cup white vinegar

2 tablespoons fresh lime juice

2 garlic cloves, finely chopped

Bring the water to a boil in a small saucepan and add the sugar, stirring to dissolve. Remove from the heat and allow to cool. Add all the remaining ingredients.

MINIATURE SPRING ROLLS
Nom Kriep

MAKES 40 TO 45
MINIATURE SPRING ROLLS

½ cup peanuts, roasted and coarsely ground

½ pound ground pork

1½ tablespoons sugar

1 teaspoon salt

¼ cup cold water

2 tablespoons all-purpose flour

1 package rice paper spring roll wrappers
(preferably triangular, 6 inches to a side)

4 cups vegetable oil

These Cambodian spring rolls (also called *lot*) are thinner and crisper than the Vietnamese-style *rouleaux*, and their flavor of roasted peanuts and pork comes through without any distraction from greens or dipping sauce. When I was growing up, we used to serve these rolls with other dishes like Grilled Beef with Lemongrass Paste (page 53) at cocktail parties for my father's guests with great success. Rolling up the filling is easy once you get the hang of it: just remember to keep the rice paper smooth and the edges neatly tucked in so the spring rolls do not burn while frying.

Combine the peanuts in a bowl with the pork, sugar and salt and blend thoroughly. Set aside.

To make a paste for sealing the spring rolls, in a small pan, slowly add the water to the flour, stirring continuously to avoid lumps. Cook over medium-high heat, stirring, until thickened, about 2 minutes. Remove from the heat and allow to cool.

Lay out a kitchen towel on a work surface. Dip several of the spring roll wrappers at a time into a shallow bowl of warm water and spread them out on the towel to soften, 1 to 2 minutes. Moisten more wrappers as needed as you prepare the spring rolls.

Place one of the wrappers with a tip pointing away from you. Using 1½ teaspoons of the pork mixture, make a small sausage link about 2½ inches long and ½ inch thick and lay it out across the middle of the wrapper (see the illustrations on page 47). Fold the right and left sides of the wrapper toward the center. Fold the bottom of the wrapper over the pork roll and roll up. Spread a small amount of the flour-and-water paste on the tip of the wrapper and finish rolling; press to seal. Continue to make the spring rolls until you have used up all the filling; you should be able to make 45 to 50. Leftover wrappers can be tightly wrapped and stored for later use.

Heat the oil in a large pot or deep-fryer over medium-high heat to 350°F; a cube of bread tossed in will sizzle and quickly brown. (The temperature is important: if the oil is too hot, the wrapper will cook before the filling is done; if the oil is not hot enough, the rolls will absorb the oil and become greasy.) Add about 10 spring rolls at a time and cook, stirring occasionally, until crisp and brown, 4 to 5 minutes. (Don't worry if the spring rolls stick together; when the wrappers are no longer wet, they will break apart easily.)

Remove the spring rolls from the oil with a slotted spoon as they are done and drain on paper tow-els. Allow to cool slightly and serve.

RED PORK WITH COCONUT MILK ON CRISPY RICE OR FRENCH BREAD
Nataing

SERVES 6 TO 8

Customarily, this mixture of ground pork enriched by coconut milk and peanuts and turned a beautiful red from spicy peppers is served over cakes of Crispy Rice. But because the Crispy Rice takes some time to prepare, when I'm in a hurry, I serve the pork over slices of French bread that have been deep-fried quickly in oil; it's nearly as good that way. I also like to cut the richness a little by serving *Nataing* with something acidic, the obvious choice being any of the traditional pickles in this book. This is one dish I like better without fish sauce, so I add additional salt, which helps to balance the appetizer's sweetness.

¼ cup vegetable oil

½ pound ground pork

1 dried New Mexico chili, soaked, seeded, deveined and ground to a powder (or 1–1½ tablespoons paprika)

8 garlic cloves, thinly sliced

1 large shallot, thinly sliced

1 cup unsweetened coconut milk

¼ cup sugar

¼ cup peanuts, roasted and coarsely ground

1 tablespoon fish sauce (optional)

½ teaspoon salt (if not using fish sauce, use 1½ teaspoons)

Crispy Rice (page 203) or 1 medium baguette, cut slightly less than ½ inch thick and deep-fried in oil until golden

Heat the oil in a large skillet over medium-high heat. Add the pork and chili powder and cook, stirring to break apart the meat, for about 3 minutes. Add the garlic and shallot, then stir in the coconut milk, sugar, peanuts, fish sauce (if using) and salt. Cook for another 10 minutes, or until the pork is no longer pink, the garlic and shallots have softened and the flavors have blended. Serve warm with Crispy Rice or bread.

GRILLED BEEF WITH LEMONGRASS PASTE
Saiko Ang Kroeung

MAKES 16 SKEWERS

16 wooden or metal skewers

PASTE
1 stalk lemongrass, thinly sliced
2 large shallots, coarsely chopped
5 garlic cloves, coarsely chopped
2 kaffir lime leaves, deveined
⅛ teaspoon turmeric
¼ cup water

3 tablespoons vegetable oil
1½ tablespoons sugar
1 teaspoon salt
1¼ pounds boneless sirloin steak, cut into pieces 1½
    inches long by 1¼ inches wide and ¼ inch thick
⅓ cup peanuts, roasted and finely ground

TO MAKE THE PASTE: Blend all the ingredients in
a blender until smooth, 2 to 3 minutes. Combine the paste in
a bowl with the oil, sugar and salt.

Add sirloin and stir to coat thoroughly with the
paste. Allow to marinate for at least an hour
at room temperature or as long
as overnight in the re-
frigerator.

You can find beef grilled on
skewers almost anywhere
in Cambodia, but the street
version is not nearly as
tasty as this homemade
treat, which is marinated in
a deliciously aromatic,
lemony paste. Grilled Beef
with Lemongrass Paste is
wonderful not just for
appetizers but also as an
entree, served with rice, a
pickled side dish, such as
Red Pepper Relish (page
255), and a salad. Because
the paste used for this dish
is also used for Pork
Brochettes with Shredded
Coconut (page 58), you
might want to make a
double batch of it and
freeze the second half for
later use.

Preheat the grill or broiler, positioning a rack about 4 inches from the heat. Dividing the pieces evenly, thread the meat onto wooden or metal skewers. Grill to a medium doneness, 2 to 3 minutes per side, being careful not to overcook.

Sprinkle the beef with the ground roasted peanuts and serve hot.

CAMBODIAN GINGER-CURED BEEF
Saiko Niet

MAKES 10 TO 20 SLICES

1 pound boneless top round, sliced ⅛ inch thick, across the grain
3 tablespoons sugar
1½ tablespoons peeled, finely chopped ginger
2 teaspoons salt
1 tablespoon vegetable oil (if cooking on the stove-top)

——————

Combine the meat with the sugar, ginger and salt in a bowl and stir to coat thoroughly. Lay the pieces out on a rack and place in a warm spot to cure for at least 8 hours and up to 24 hours. The meat will turn purplish red, with a light sheen to it, and will feel somewhat leathery.

TO COOK ON THE STOVETOP: Heat the oil in a large skillet over medium-high heat. Cook the beef in batches, pressing down on the slices for even cooking, about 1½ minutes per side.

TO GRILL OR BROIL: Preheat the grill or broiler, positioning a rack about 2 inches away from the flame. Cook for 1½ minutes per side.

Serve warm or at room temperature.

This sweet, ginger-flavored cured beef makes a memorable appetizer served with drinks and pickles. It's great as part of a meal, and it's also delicious to snack on throughout the day. In Cambodia, where the sun is hot, the beef cures quickly in the sugar and ginger, and we grill it very close to the flame for a short time so it doesn't dry out. Although the recipe calls for top round, I have always made this jerky with whatever kind of meat I have left over from cooking — nothing fancy. The cured beef can be stored in the refrigerator for several days or in the freezer for about six months, although I've never had anything left to store.

SPICY CHICKEN WINGS
Slab Mouan Kroeung

SERVES 6 TO 8

Lemongrass adds a wonderfully full flavor to chicken, and the longer you can marinate these wings, the better. I like to serve them with a bowl of Cambodian sour pickles — particularly Mixed Vegetable Pickles (page 256) — and a cold drink, but they are also terrific just by themselves. In Cambodia, cooks grill these wings, but I think they taste great broiled (use a rack that lets the grease drip away) or deep-fried.

PASTE
3 tablespoons sliced lemongrass
4 garlic cloves, coarsely chopped
1 medium shallot, coarsely chopped
1 tablespoon peeled, coarsely chopped galangal
½ teaspoon paprika
¼ teaspoon turmeric
½ cup water

2 tablespoons peanuts, roasted and finely ground
2 tablespoons fish sauce
3 tablespoons sugar
1 teaspoon salt
1½–2 pounds chicken wings
4 cups vegetable oil (if deep-frying)

TO MAKE THE PASTE: Blend all the ingredients in a blender until smooth, 2 to 3 minutes.

In a bowl, combine the paste with the peanuts, fish sauce, sugar and salt. Marinate the chicken in this sauce for at least 20 minutes at room temperature or as long as overnight in the refrigerator.

TO GRILL OR BROIL: Preheat the grill or broiler, positioning a rack about 4 inches from the heat. Cook the wings, turning occasionally, until dark brown, 15 to 20 minutes; watch carefully so as not to burn.

TO DEEP-FRY: Heat the oil to 350°F in a large pot or deep-fryer (a cube of bread tossed in will sizzle and quickly brown). Add the wings in batches and fry for 10 to 12 minutes, turning occasionally, until golden all over. Remove with a slotted spoon, drain on paper towels and serve hot.

PORK BROCHETTES WITH SHREDDED COCONUT
Saik Chrouk Ch'ranouitk

MAKES 16 SKEWERS

16 wooden or metal skewers

¼ cup Lemongrass Paste (see page 53)
½ cup freshly grated coconut or packaged
     unsweetened shredded coconut
1 tablespoon sugar
½ teaspoon salt
1 pound pork tenderloin, pork loin or fresh ham, cut
     into pieces 1½ inches long by 1¼ inches wide
     and ½ inch thick

Combine the lemongrass paste in a bowl with the shredded coconut, sugar and salt, mixing thoroughly. Add the pieces of pork and stir to coat thoroughly with the paste. Let marinate for at least an hour at room temperature or as long as overnight in the refrigerator.

Preheat the grill or broiler, positioning a rack about 4 inches from the heat. Dividing the pieces of meat evenly, thread them onto wooden or metal skewers. Grill for 3 to 4 minutes per side, until the pork is nicely browned on the outside and just cooked through — but not dry — on the inside. Serve immediately.

Although I had these brochettes only two or three times at very fancy occasions while I was growing up, I remembered the way they tasted for years. The grilled pork seasoned with the lemony paste and sprinkled with freshly grated coconut captured my imagination. I couldn't find anyone who knew how to make them or even what they were called, so I had to reconstruct the recipe on my own, but I think the experimentation paid off. The brochettes go well with Cucumber Relish (page 257) and cold drinks, and you can transform them into an entree by serving them with rice.

FRIED CORN CAKES
Poat Chien

MAKES ABOUT 12 CAKES

This Cambodian version of corn fritters combines grated coconut with thinly sliced corn kernels in crisply fried little pancakes. In Cambodia, we like to eat them as a snack at any time of day, but they would also do well as a side dish for a Western meal. American corn is less starchy than corn that grows in Cambodia, so these cakes need the glutinous rice flour to hold the mixture together, and because the corn here is somewhat sweet, you will need to adjust the amount of sugar to the sweetness of the particular corn you are using and to your own taste.

3 ears corn
3 tablespoons freshly grated coconut or packaged
   unsweetened shredded coconut
⅓ cup unsweetened coconut milk
¼ cup glutinous rice flour
2–3 tablespoons sugar, or to taste
¼ teaspoon salt
2 tablespoons vegetable oil

With a very sharp knife, make several passes across the kernels of the corn until you're down to the bare cob, then scrape against the cob to get out the milky starch. (If using a mandoline or other scraper, pass the cob back and forth over the cutting blades several times.) You should have 2½ to 3 cups.

Combine the corn, coconut, coconut milk, rice flour, sugar and salt in a bowl, stirring and pressing the corn with the back of a spoon to release as much of the starchy liquid as possible, about 5 minutes.

Heat the oil in a skillet over medium-high heat. For each cake, spoon about 1 tablespoon of batter into the skillet and cook until well browned, 3 to 4 minutes per side. Drain on paper towels. Serve hot.

STEAMED YUCA WITH COCONUT DIPPING SAUCE
Dom Lung Cheuh

SERVES 4 TO 6

1¾ pounds yuca

DIPPING SAUCE
⅔ cup unsweetened coconut milk
2½ tablespoons sugar
1 teaspoon salt
3 tablespoons thinly sliced scallions (green part
   only)
1 teaspoon all-purpose flour
1 tablespoon cold water

Steamed Yuca makes a nice appetizer to serve with pickles and grilled meat, such as Pork Brochettes with Shredded Coconut (page 58) or Grilled Beef with Lemongrass Paste (page 53). The yuca is starchy and filling, and the coconut sauce is slightly salty but also sweet, with an added oniony flavor from the scallions, making this tasty, satisfying and popular snack the Cambodian equivalent of french fries with ketchup. This recipe is even simpler to prepare if you have a microwave.

Fill the bottom of a steamer with water and bring to a boil over high heat. Peel the yuca and cut into spears 4 inches long and about ½ inch thick, removing the tough center core. Place the yuca in the top of the steamer, cover and steam over boiling water for 30 to 40 minutes, replenishing water as needed, until tender.

Or put the yuca in a microwave-safe dish, cover with plastic wrap and heat in the microwave on high for 8 to 10 minutes.

MEANWHILE, MAKE THE DIPPING SAUCE: Combine the coconut milk with the sugar, salt and scallions in a medium saucepan and set over medium-high heat. Mix the flour and water in a small bowl, then stir into the coconut-milk mixture and simmer, stirring, until thickened, about 2 minutes.

Serve the yuca warm or at room temperature with the dipping sauce.

GRILLED CORN
Poat Dot

Cambodians slather freshly cooked corn with a sweet and salty sauce, eating it as street food, not at home as part of the meal. This recipe is so simple that it hardly seems to warrant being written down, yet it would be such a loss if it were to disappear. This sauce would be terrific served with other grilled foods, like Grilled Marinated Pork Ribs (page 148) or Grilled Fish (page 158), and it's a perfect side dish for any light summer meal.

SERVES 2 TO 4

4 ears corn
2 tablespoons vegetable oil
1 scallion, thinly sliced
1 tablespoon water
1 tablespoon sugar
1 teaspoon fish sauce
½ teaspoon salt

Prepare the corn by steaming or grilling, as preferred.

Meanwhile, heat the oil in a small pan over high heat. Add the remaining ingredients and stir-fry until the scallion begins to wilt, about 30 seconds. Brush this sauce over the hot corn and serve.

BROILED CLAMS WITH LEMONGRASS
Nyeu Kroeung

SERVES 4

PASTE

1 dried New Mexico chili, soaked, seeded and
    deveined
1 tablespoon thinly sliced lemongrass
2 garlic cloves, coarsely chopped
1 large shallot, coarsely chopped
5 kaffir lime leaves, deveined
1 teaspoon peeled, coarsely chopped galangal
2 tablespoons chopped fresh cilantro stems
¼ teaspoon turmeric
1 bird's eye chili
½ cup water

1 dozen medium littleneck clams in the shell
2 tablespoons vegetable oil
¼ cup unsweetened coconut milk
2 tablespoons sugar
1 teaspoon salt
1 teaspoon fish sauce
¼ cup peanuts, roasted and coarsely ground
Cilantro sprigs, for garnish

These tender clams, served on the half-shell in a richly flavored coconut sauce, are considered a sophisticated and exotic appetizer even in Cambodia. There is a big difference between the clams in this country and the freshwater ones we have at home, but I think the method of broiling littlenecks that my son-in-law Gérard and I came up with comes close to the authentic taste. This dish is so rich that even when I serve it as an entree, three clams per person are enough. If I do serve the clams with rice as an entree, I increase the salt to 2 teaspoons to keep them from tasting bland.

TO MAKE THE PASTE: Blend all the ingredients in a blender until smooth, 2 to 3 minutes.

Scrub and shuck the clams. Lay out half the shells on a broiler pan and place one clam in each shell.

Heat the oil in a large pan over medium-high heat. Add the paste, coconut milk, sugar, salt and fish sauce. Cook, stirring, until the sauce has thickened to the consistency of ketchup, about 8 minutes. Spoon the sauce over the clams and sprinkle with the ground peanuts.

Preheat the grill or broiler, positioning a rack about 6 inches from the heat. Grill or broil the clams until heated through but still tender, 4 to 6 minutes. Top with sprigs of cilantro and serve immediately.

STICKY RICE TOPPED WITH SHELLFISH
Bai Domnap Muk B'kong

SERVES 4 TO 8

Cheesecloth

2 cups glutinous rice, soaked in warm water for at
    least 2 hours, preferably overnight, and drained
½ cup unsweetened coconut milk
2 teaspoons salt
½ teaspoon turmeric
1½ pounds freshwater lobster (with coral), shelled
    and deveined, or ¾ pound shrimp, shelled and
    deveined
2 tablespoons vegetable oil
2½ tablespoons sugar
12 kaffir lime leaves, deveined and julienned
Banana leaves or lettuce leaves (optional)

Looking for all the world like *petits fours,* these beautiful little rice cakes are showcase appetizers for special occasions. The rich lobster or shrimp, the coconut milk and the aromatic rice complement one another perfectly, and the brilliant yellow and orange layers topped with dark green threads of lime leaves are striking. In Cambodia, these snacks would be served in individual little holders made of banana leaves, which add a wonderful fragrance.

Fill the bottom of a large steamer with water and bring to a boil. Line the upper portion of the steamer with a double layer of cheesecloth and spread the rice out over the cloth. Cover the pot and steam for about 15 minutes, or until the rice is shiny and there is no crunch left in the kernels when you bite into them.

Mix the coconut milk, 1 teaspoon of the salt and the turmeric together in a small bowl and spread over the top of the rice. Lifting up the edges of the cheesecloth one area at a time, thoroughly intermingle the rice with the sauce until the yellow color is evenly dispersed. Cover and steam for 10 minutes more.

Reserving the coral (if using lobster), process the lobster or shrimp meat in a food processor or blender by pulsing for two 3-second intervals: the mixture should be somewhat coarse in texture. You should have about 1⅓ cups.

Heat the oil in a large skillet over medium-high heat. Add the lobster or shrimp and cook, stirring and pressing down to break up any clumps, until pink, 6 to 7 minutes. Stir in the sugar and the remaining 1 teaspoon salt. The shellfish is done when all the liquid has evaporated. (If you are using freshwater lobster, now is the time to add the coral, stirring well — it will turn the mixture a bright reddish orange.) Remove from the heat.

To serve, spread the rice out in the bottom of a 13-by-9-inch serving dish by pressing down with the back of a spoon or your fingers until it is evenly distributed and holds together. Do the same with the shellfish mixture, to create two layers that stick together, and then sprinkle with the julienned kaffir lime leaves. Cut the layers into squares or diamonds and serve them directly from the dish.

Alternatively, you can stamp out shapes with cookie cutters. Serve the rice shapes on top of banana leaves or lettuce if you like, for an even prettier effect.

SOUPS

SOUP IS ANOTHER CULINARY CATEGORY THAT DOESN'T TRANSLATE directly from Cambodian cuisine. We certainly do cook foods in large quantities of liquids — in fact, we cook a great number of dishes by this method — but we don't think about them in the same way that Westerners do. For instance, we serve soup at almost every meal as one of the entrees, not set off from the other foods. When we do have soup alone, it's as a snack or for breakfast — a hot, filling meal before the day heats up, served with cool fresh herbs and bean sprouts.

We also *eat* our soups differently: for example, instead of using a spoon to get the solids and liquids of Lemongrass Pork Soup (page 90) into the same mouthful, we're more likely to remove pieces of the pork ribs and watercress to a plate to eat separately and then use some of the broth as a sauce for our rice. After that, we might drink the rest of the broth by itself, as though having tea with our meal.

Cambodian soups tend to fall into two main categories, known in Khmer as *s'ngao* and *somlah*. A *s'ngao* is a simple clear broth with a relatively small number of ingredients and a straightforward taste, like Spicy Chicken Soup (page 83). A *somlah*, on the other hand, is made with a spice paste, which tends to make it more complex in flavor and thicker — particularly if it includes coconut milk, which it often does. When tamarind juice is added to a *somlah*, as it is in Lemongrass Pork Soup and White Fish Soup with Young Winter Melon (page 100), it becomes a *somlah machou,* or sour soup.

In addition to broth, some of the more traditional forms of soup include rice or noodles, small amounts of meat and fish, preserved vegetables and fresh herbs, fried garlic, chilies and a host of other possible garnishes. The number of last-minute ingredients for a traditional Khmer soup is very large indeed, which is one of the reasons that most people buy their *K'tieu,* Classic Noodle Soup, or *B'baw Mouan,* Essential Rice Soup, at a soup stand instead of making it at home. But if I had to choose only a couple of recipes to represent the essence of Cambodian cuisine, I would almost certainly pick these classics, which seem to me somehow to capture the Cambodian soul.

SPICY DAIKON SOUP
S'ngao Chai Tao

SERVES 4

8 cups water

1 teaspoon salt

1 pound spareribs or baby back ribs, cut across the
   bone into 1-inch pieces (a butcher can do this for
   you), then cut between the bones

3 garlic cloves, smashed

6 small black fungi, soaked in warm water
   for 15 minutes and drained (or 1 large black
   fungus, soaked, drained and cut into 6 pieces)

1 pound daikon, peeled, cut in half lengthwise
   and sliced crosswise ¼ inch thick

3 tablespoons fish sauce

1 tablespoon dried shrimp, rinsed and drained

1 teaspoon sugar

¼ teaspoon freshly ground pepper

1 scallion, cut into 1-inch pieces

Cilantro sprigs, for garnish

In this clear broth soup, black mushrooms provide an earthy backdrop for the slightly pungent, oniony flavor and crunchy texture of the white radish called daikon. Daikon is very popular in Khmer cuisine — a testimony to the influence of Chinese culture — and this soup is one of my favorite ways to eat it. I also enjoy how the little bits of dried shrimp go off like salty, fishy flares that light up the soup and keep it lively.

Bring the water and salt to a boil in a large stockpot. Add the ribs and garlic. Return to the boil, skim, lower the heat and simmer, partially covered, for 25 to 30 minutes.

Add the fungi, daikon, fish sauce, dried shrimp and sugar and cook until the daikon is tender, about 15 minutes more.

Stir in the pepper and scallion, garnish with cilantro and serve with rice.

BEAN THREAD
NOODLE SOUP
Somlah Mee Souah

SERVES 4

¼ cup small dried black fungus

15–20 dried lilies (about ½ ounce)

3–4 ounces bean thread noodles

2 tablespoons vegetable oil

4 garlic cloves, smashed

¼ pound ground pork

1 teaspoon salt

1 teaspoon sugar

4 cups chicken broth (6 cups if serving with rice)

15 small dried shrimp (about 1 tablespoon), rinsed
    and drained

1 tablespoon fish sauce

2 scallions, cut into 2-inch pieces

¼ teaspoon freshly ground pepper

The fact that you can make this soup in under 15 minutes should be almost recommendation enough, but add to that the rich flavor of the pork highlighted by the garlic and shrimp and the filling quality of the noodles, and you have something very special. This soup can be served as a main course with rice (in which case, you should add another 2 cups of broth) or as an accompaniment to grilled fish or chicken, with Cambodian pickles. You need to serve it quickly, though, as the noodles have a tendency to expand, absorbing all the broth, if they sit for long.

Soak the black fungus, dried lilies and bean thread noodles in separate bowls in warm water to cover for 10 minutes, then drain. Cut the noodles into 3-inch lengths, using scissors, and set aside.

Heat the oil in a wok or large skillet over medium-high heat and sauté the garlic until golden brown, 5 to 10 seconds. Stir in the pork, breaking apart any clumps, then stir in the salt and sugar. Add the chicken broth, turn the heat up to high and as the broth comes to a boil, add the shrimp, black fungus, dried lilies and fish sauce. When the broth reaches a boil, lower the heat to a simmer.

Add the noodles to the broth. Cook, stirring, for about 1 minute. Remove from the heat, add the scallions and pepper, stir and serve at once.

BAMBOO SHOOT SOUP
Somlah Prahah Tompeang

SERVES 4

2 garlic cloves

2 pieces rhizome, each 2–3 inches long

5–6 cups chicken broth

1¼ pounds fresh bamboo shoots, peeled, sliced and parboiled (page 284), or ¾ pound canned whole shoots, thinly sliced (3–4 cups)

2 tablespoons fish sauce

2 teaspoons salt

2 teaspoons sugar

1½ teaspoons jasmine rice, rinsed

1½ teaspoons *prahok* (optional)

¼ pound pork tenderloin or boneless pork butt, thinly sliced

½ cup unsweetened coconut milk (optional)

¾ pound catfish fillets, cut into strips 4 inches long by 2 inches wide

Handful of chili leaves or fresh spinach leaves

Sliced red bell pepper, for garnish

Pound the garlic and rhizome together with a mortar and pestle until well blended or grind in a mini-chop.

In a large pot, add the chicken broth, bamboo shoots, fish sauce, salt, sugar, rice, *prahok* (if using), and the garlic-rhizome mixture. Bring to a boil, reduce the heat to low and cook for about 10 minutes, until the bamboo shoots are tender and the rice is the texture of porridge. Add the pork and coconut milk (if using) and simmer for 20 minutes more. Add the catfish and cook until tender, about 5 minutes. Remove from the heat, stir in the chili or spinach leaves and serve immediately, garnished with red pepper slices.

This soup is a taste tribute to the delicate flavor of fresh bamboo shoots, but in this country, it's not always easy to get fresh shoots. I've tried a lot of different bamboo products imported from Asia and, to my surprise, have found that canned whole shoots are really quite good. Another innovation for me came during our recent trip to Cambodia, when my daughters, Launa and Nadsa, tasted this soup served with coconut milk — a regional variation in the northwest — and liked it better than the one that I make with a plain chicken broth. You can try it both ways to discover your own preference. Chili leaves, which you can buy in a Southeast Asian market or strip off a pepper plant (hot or sweet) in your own garden, add a nice sharp note to the soup, and, like the spinach leaves I suggest as a substitute, a nice color, as well. The small amount of rice gives just the right thickness to the soup.

COCONUT MILK SOUP WITH BAMBOO SHOOTS
Somlah K'tih Tompeang

SERVES 4

PASTE

14 garlic cloves, coarsely chopped

4 dried New Mexico chilies, soaked, seeded and deveined

1 tablespoon peeled, coarsely chopped galangal

2 pieces rhizome, each 2–3 inches long

14 garlic cloves, coarsely chopped

1 teaspoon shrimp paste

¼ teaspoon turmeric

½ cup water

5 teaspoons vegetable oil

1¾ cups unsweetened coconut milk

1 whole chicken (about 1½ pounds), cut into 2-inch pieces

2 tablespoons fish sauce

5 teaspoons sugar

1 tablespoon salt

2 stalks lemongrass, bottom halves only, smashed

1½ cups water

1 pound fresh bamboo shoots, peeled, sliced and parboiled (page 284), or ½ pound canned whole shoots, thinly sliced

6 kaffir lime leaves

This thick, rich soup, heavily influenced by the spice traditions of India, features all the major flavorings of the Cambodian culinary palate: garlic, lemongrass, kaffir lime leaves and the gingery galangal and rhizome. It also brings together the coconut milk of elite Thai cuisine and the mild, tender bamboo shoots so prominent in the cuisine of neighboring Laos.

TO MAKE THE PASTE: Blend all the ingredients in a blender until smooth, 2 to 3 minutes. Set aside.

In a large pan, heat the oil over medium-high heat. Add ¼ cup of the coconut milk and cook until the oil separates from the milk, 3 to 4 minutes. Add the paste and cook, stirring constantly, for another 3 to 4 minutes, until the flavors are well developed.

Stir the chicken into the sauce to coat, then add the remaining 1½ cups coconut milk, fish sauce, sugar, salt, lemongrass and water. Bring to a boil, reduce the heat to low and simmer until the chicken is almost tender, 10 to 15 minutes. Add the bamboo shoots and kaffir lime leaves and cook for another 15 minutes.

You can serve this soup immediately, but standing time only improves its flavors, particularly as the essence of the kaffir lime leaves is released. Serve with rice.

ESSENTIAL RICE SOUP
B'baw Mouan

SERVES 4 TO 6 GENEROUSLY

4 quarts water

I teaspoon salt

2 pounds chicken pieces (whole legs work well)

2 cups jasmine rice

20 garlic cloves

½ cup plus I tablespoon vegetable oil

3 tablespoons fish sauce, plus more for serving

2 teaspoons sugar

½ teaspoon salt

¼ cup dried shrimp, rinsed and drained

½ pound mung bean sprouts

4 scallions, thinly sliced on the diagonal

½ cup chopped fresh cilantro leaves and stems

⅓ cup preserved cabbage

Lime wedges

Thinly sliced bird's eye chilies

Its plain name can't possibly begin to sum up the spectacular appeal of this soup, which Cambodians happily eat every day, particularly for breakfast. The base is a simple rice-and-chicken-broth porridge. But then diners add fried garlic, shrimp, cilantro, lime and a host of other toothsome garnishes to make just the meal that they want. Whatever you choose to add to the soup, be sure to sauté the rice before putting it in the broth, as this step contributes a lot of flavor. I recommend using kosher or organic free-range chickens for the same reason.

Bring the water to a boil in a large stockpot and add the salt and chicken. Return to a boil, reduce the heat and simmer, partially covered, for 25 to 30 minutes or until the chicken is tender. Set aside to cool.

While the chicken is cooking, rinse the rice in a strainer by running water over it and drain.

Smash and coarsely chop 2 of the garlic cloves. In a large skillet, heat I tablespoon of the oil over high heat and sauté the chopped garlic for 5 to 10 seconds, until golden brown. Add the rice and cook, stirring to break up any clumps, until the rice loses its translucence, begins to fluff and starts to brown slightly, 5 to 6 minutes.

Add the rice mixture to the broth and return to a boil.

Lower the heat and simmer for 15 minutes, stirring occasionally. Add the fish sauce, sugar and salt and continue cooking and stirring for another 15 minutes, until the rice begins to become mushy, almost like a puree. (If the soup gets too thick, you can always add more water.)

Meanwhile, coarsely chop the remaining 18 garlic cloves. Heat the remaining ½ cup oil in the skillet over medium-high heat and fry the garlic until brown but not burned, 1 to 2 minutes. Remove the garlic with a slotted spoon and set aside.

Remove the skin from the cooled chicken, shred the meat with your fingers and return it to the soup. Put the dried shrimp, mung bean sprouts, scallions, cilantro, preserved cabbage, lime wedges and sliced chili peppers (and anything else you'd like) on a platter.

Serve the soup in one large tureen or four to six individual bowls, adding ingredients from the platter as desired. A common preparation is to stir the dried shrimp into the soup, add a handful of bean sprouts around the edge of the tureen or bowls, sprinkle the scallions and cilantro in the center and top with fried garlic. Add the preserved cabbage, lime juice and chilies to taste.

CLASSIC NOODLE SOUP
K'tieu

In Cambodia, this soup is
almost a national dish. On
any corner in the capital
city of Phnom Penh, for
example, you might see
people sitting or squatting
by small stands and tiny
hole-in-the-wall eateries,
slurping up the slender rice
noodles from the broth,
which is spiced with fried
garlic and bright red bird's
eye chilies, some shrimp,
perhaps, and a bit of meat.
Because it's so readily
available on the street, we
don't tend to make this
soup at home, though it's
really not difficult. You
make a basic broth — either
pork or chicken — and then
prepare the seasonings and
garnishes to be added; it's
the variety that gives the
soup its splendid taste and
wide appeal. A bowl of
K'tieu is like nothing else.
See the photograph on
page 81.

SERVES 4 TO 6 GENEROUSLY

5 quarts water

4 pounds pork or chicken bones (pork are
    preferable)

1 small onion

1 carrot, peeled

½ pound pork tenderloin, pork loin or fresh ham

¼ cup vegetable oil

20 garlic cloves, finely chopped

¼ cup sugar

4 teaspoons salt

½ pound ground pork

1 pound rice noodles (as thin as possible), soaked in
    warm water for 10 minutes and drained

SEASONINGS AND GARNISHES

Vegetable oil

Soy sauce

½ cup preserved cabbage

4 scallions, sliced ¼ inch thick

½ pound mung bean sprouts

½ cup or more dried shrimp, rinsed and drained

1 bunch cilantro, leaves and stems, torn into
    bite-sized pieces (about 2 cups)

Freshly ground pepper

Sliced bird's eye chilies

Cooked, shelled shrimp (about 3 per person)

Bring the water to a boil in a large stockpot and add the
bones, onion and carrot. Return to a boil, skim off any froth,
reduce the heat to low and simmer for 2 to 3 hours, until all
the flavor of the bones is released into the broth. Strain the
broth and discard the bones and vegetables.

Meanwhile, simmer the pork or ham in a medium pot in water to cover for about 30 minutes, or until tender. Drain, thinly slice and set aside.

Heat the oil in a small skillet over medium heat and fry the garlic until well browned, 2 to 3 minutes. Remove from the oil and set aside.

Once you've strained the pork or chicken broth, add the sugar and salt, stir to dissolve and turn off the heat. Remove ½ cup of the broth to a small saucepan and cover the remaining broth. Simmer the ground pork in the small saucepan of broth over medium-high heat until cooked through, 2 to 3 minutes, breaking it apart as it cooks. Drain the pork and set aside.

To prepare the noodles, choose a medium-sized pot that can accommodate a strainer and fill it three-quarters full with water. Bring the water to a boil. Put the strainer in place so that it dips into the water and add the soaked noodles. Shake the strainer to make sure the water reaches all the noodles, let stand for about 2 seconds and then remove the strainer.

Divide the noodles among large individual soup bowls and add to each 1½ teaspoons oil and about 2 teaspoons soy sauce, mixing well.

Put the remaining seasonings and garnishes and the sliced

pork, fried garlic and ground pork in three small bowls on the table.

From here on out, people can create a bowl of soup to suit their own tastes, but the following is a general guideline: In the center of the bowl, on top of the noodles, put 2 table-spoons cooked ground pork and a few slices of the cooked pork. Around the edge of the bowl, in small piles, arrange 1½ teaspoons preserved cabbage, 1 teaspoon each of the fried garlic and scallions and a mound of bean sprouts. Spoon enough broth over all just to cover and sprinkle with some dried shrimp, cilantro, ¼ teaspoon pepper, chilies and the cooked shrimp. Use chopsticks to mix the ingredients together, and enjoy.

CAMBODIAN BEEF AND BROTH
Khar Ko

SERVES 4

This recipe produces what I consider to be the ultimate beef broth. One of the reasons it's so good is that it's made with a cut of beef that has lots of bones for flavor, but the onions and garlic roasted with their skins on also contribute an enormous amount of depth. I've found that carrots taste great in this soup, and I generally add them along with the garlic and onion. Served with a simple salad and good bread, the soup makes the perfect cold-weather meal.

9 cups water
1 teaspoon salt
2½ pounds beef shanks
1 small onion (¼ pound), unpeeled, rinsed
2 garlic cloves, unpeeled
2–3 carrots, cut into 2-inch pieces (optional)
1 tablespoon fish sauce, plus more for serving
2 teaspoons sugar
¼ cup loosely packed fresh basil leaves, for garnish
1 scallion, thinly sliced, for garnish
Lime wedges
Thinly sliced bird's eye chilies

Bring the water and salt to boil in a large stockpot and add the beef. Return to a boil.

Meanwhile, preheat the broiler. Put the unpeeled onion and garlic cloves under the broiler and cook, turning often, until their skins are well browned (don't let them burn); the onion should take 2 to 3 minutes, the garlic about 1. Add to the broth, along with the beef and the carrots.

When the broth reaches a boil, skim off any froth, lower the heat to medium and simmer, partially covered, until the meat has fallen off the bones and the broth has absorbed all the flavor, about 2 hours.

Stir in the fish sauce and sugar and pour into individual bowls, dividing the bones among the bowls if you wish, as Cambodians do. Garnish with the basil and scallion and serve with small bowls of lime wedges, chilies and more fish sauce.

SPICY CHICKEN SOUP
S'ngao Mouan

SERVES 4

8 cups water

1½ pounds chicken parts (preferably 1 whole breast
   and 1 whole leg)

1 stalk lemongrass, bulb split

2 garlic cloves, smashed

2 tablespoons fish sauce, plus more for serving

4 teaspoons salt

2 teaspoons sugar

¼ cup fresh lime juice (1–2 limes)

2 scallions, cut diagonally into 1-inch pieces

Handful of fresh basil leaves, coarsely chopped

Thinly sliced bird's eye chilies

Bring the water to a boil in a small stockpot and add the chicken, lemongrass and garlic. Return to a boil and skim the surface thoroughly. Reduce the heat and simmer, partly covered, until the chicken is tender, 25 to 30 minutes. Add the fish sauce, salt and sugar.

Remove the chicken from the simmering broth and set aside on a plate. Cool just enough so you can shred the meat from the bones with your fingers. Return the shredded meat to the pot to heat through.

Remove the lemongrass from the broth and discard. Stir in the lime juice, scallions and basil. Transfer the soup to a tureen or four individual bowls and serve immediately with rice, with sliced chilies and more fish sauce on the side.

This is the quintessential Cambodian clear broth soup — simple, light and flavorful, with the bright, fresh taste of lime, scallion and basil. The Cambodian way to eat this soup is to fish the chicken and greens out of the broth, put them onto a plate with rice and eat them "dry," adding chilies and fish sauce to taste and drinking the broth separately. But needless to say, you should feel free to have this soup "wet," enjoying all of its ingredients together, though I would certainly recommend serving rice on the side. Spicy Chicken Soup is considered appropriate at any time of the day, at any meal or all by itself.

EMERALD SOUP
Somlah Marakot

SERVES 4

PASTE

1 stalk lemongrass, thinly sliced
8 kaffir lime leaves, deveined
5 garlic cloves, coarsely chopped
1 large shallot, coarsely chopped
2 teaspoons peeled, coarsely chopped galangal
⅔ cup water

2–2½ pounds chicken parts (2 legs and 1 whole breast)
½ pound poblano chilies (about 3 large), seeded and deveined
¾ pound cubanelle peppers (about 3 large), seeded and deveined
¼ cup vegetable oil
3½ cups unsweetened coconut milk
3 tablespoons fish sauce
1½ tablespoons sugar
2½ teaspoons salt
1 teaspoon shrimp paste
1 cup unsalted chicken broth
1 cup fresh or frozen peas
Fresh basil leaves, for garnish
Thinly sliced bird's eye chilies

This beautiful pale green soup, named for the precious gems our country is famous for, gets its color and a lot of its flavor from poblano chilies, cubanelle peppers and peas. Coconut milk thickens and enriches the soup further and serves as a perfect background for a complexity of seasonings. In Cambodia, we would make the broth for this soup with a whole chicken, including the liver and gizzards, but American cooks may be more comfortable using legs and breasts: with either method, your aim is a flavorful broth.

TO MAKE THE PASTE: Blend all the ingredients in a blender until smooth, 2 to 3 minutes. Set aside.

With a cleaver, hack the chicken into pieces about 1½ inches in size. Cut both kinds of peppers in half lengthwise, then cut the halves on the diagonal into bite-sized slices. Set aside.

Heat the oil in a large pot over medium-high heat. Add ½ cup of the coconut milk and cook, stirring occasionally, until the oil separates from the milk, 2 to 3 minutes. Add the spice paste, stirring well, and simmer for 5 to 6 minutes more, to blend the flavors.

Add the fish sauce, sugar, salt, shrimp paste and chicken, stirring well to coat, and cook for 10 minutes. Add the broth and the remaining 3 cups coconut milk. Return to a simmer, add the peppers and peas and cook, partially covered, for another 10 to 15 minutes, or until the chicken is tender.

Garnish with basil leaves and serve with sliced bird's eye chilies and rice.

KHMER CHICKEN SOUP WITH EGGPLANT

Somlah Machou Mouan

SERVES 4

PASTE

4 dried New Mexico chilies, soaked, seeded and
   deveined
1 tablespoon sliced lemongrass
1 tablespoon peeled, coarsely chopped galangal
2 medium shallots, coarsely chopped
5 garlic cloves, coarsely chopped
½ teaspoon turmeric
4 kaffir lime leaves, deveined
1 teaspoon shrimp paste
1 cup water

2 tablespoons vegetable oil
¼ cup unsweetened coconut milk
1 pound chicken breasts, skinned, boned and meat
   sliced into ½-inch-thick strips
4 cups chicken broth (if not using organic chicken)
   or water
2 teaspoons sugar
1 teaspoon fish sauce
1 teaspoon *prahok* (optional)
1 teaspoon salt
3 cups small round Asian eggplants, trimmed and
   cut in half (or 2 medium ordinary eggplants, cut
   into
   1-inch cubes)
¼ cup tamarind juice
Handful of fresh basil leaves, for garnish

TO MAKE THE PASTE: Blend all the ingredients in

I particularly like the way
the slightly bitter taste of
the eggplant in this soup is
offset by the sweet, rich
coconut milk and the salty
fish undertones. A full-
bodied broth is desirable
here, and unless you can
get organically raised
chicken, which is more
flavorful, I suggest using
chicken broth in place of
the water. We started
serving this spicy red soup
very early on at The
Elephant Walk, and it is
extremely popular.

CLEAR DUCK SOUP WITH LIME
S'ngao Tiah Nung Kroit Tram

SERVES 6 TO 8

9 cups water

2 tablespoons fish sauce, plus more for serving

2 garlic cloves, smashed

1 tablespoon salt

1 whole duckling (5–6 pounds), rinsed, with any
   visible fat removed (particularly under the skin
   at the front and back openings)

1 preserved lime

Scallions, sliced ½ inch thick, for garnish

Cilantro sprigs, for garnish

The distinctive flavor of the preserved lime is what makes this essentially simple soup something special. The smoky taste — almost like an Earl Grey tea — perfectly complements the richness of the duck. Cambodians would tend to keep the duck whole and sear it before simmering, for extra savor. But for a soup, I think this method makes more sense: it's quicker and easier, and it still yields truly sumptuous results.

Bring the water, fish sauce, garlic and salt to a boil in a large stockpot. Meanwhile, hack the duck into 1½-to-2-inch pieces with a cleaver.

Add the duck to the pot. When the water returns to a boil, skim off any fat, reduce the heat and simmer, partially covered, until the duck is tender, about 1 hour.

Add the preserved lime to the soup and cook for another 10 minutes. When you are ready to serve the soup, press the lime with a spoon until it breaks open, making sure its flavor infuses the broth.

Transfer the soup to a tureen and garnish with scallions and cilantro. Serve with rice, with more fish sauce on the side.

LEMONGRASS PORK SOUP
Somlah Machou Kroeung Saik Chrouk

SERVES 4

PASTE

2 stalks lemongrass, thinly sliced

5 garlic cloves, coarsely chopped

1 tablespoon peeled, coarsely chopped galangal

1 large shallot, coarsely chopped

1 tablespoon chopped fresh cilantro

¼ teaspoon turmeric

4 kaffir lime leaves, deveined

⅔ cup water

2½ pounds spareribs or baby back ribs, cut into 1½-inch pieces across the bone, then cut between the bones

1 tablespoon *prahok* (optional)

5 cups water

3 tablespoons fish sauce

1½ tablespoons salt

1 tablespoon sugar

1 cup tamarind juice

1–1½ pounds Chinese watercress or regular watercress, cut into 2-inch pieces (or young winter melon or zucchini)

Julienned red bell pepper, for garnish

TO MAKE THE PASTE: Blend all the ingredients in a blender until smooth, 2 to 3 minutes.

Transfer the paste to a large pot, stir in the ribs and *prahok* (if using) and cook over medium-high heat, stirring well, for 5 to 6 minutes. Add the water, fish sauce, salt and sugar and bring to a boil over high heat. When the soup has reached a

This recipe is a great example of the kind of Cambodian soup known as *somlah machou*, with its herb paste and lightly sour taste of tamarind. These flavors serve as a backdrop for the watercress and pork ribs. Other vegetables that go well with the ribs are zucchini and young winter melon, which, unlike zucchini, has to be peeled. Cut either vegetable lengthwise in half, slice ¼ inch thick and add it half an hour before the soup is done. You may want to ask the butcher to cut the ribs into pieces for you.

boil, skim, reduce the heat and simmer, partially covered, until the ribs are tender, about 1¼ hours.

Stir in the tamarind juice and watercress, remove from the heat and serve in bowls, garnished with slices of red pepper.

CAMBODIAN SOUR SOUP WITH BEEF
Somlah Machou Saiko

When I was growing up, our cook always made this beef soup, and my favorite memory of it wasn't at the table with my family but in the kitchen, where I would sneak out and eat it with the servants. Starting with its simple but richly flavored clear broth, our cook made the soup sing by adding lots more *prahok* (fermented fish) and different cuts of meat (with more fat, I would guess) than she would ever serve to the family. The curry leaves sprinkled on top add a wonderfully smoky note, but if you can't find them, don't worry: the soup is delicious on its own.

SERVES 4

PASTE

1 stalk lemongrass, thinly sliced
6 kaffir lime leaves, deveined
2 medium shallots, coarsely chopped
1½ tablespoons peeled, coarsely chopped galangal
7 garlic cloves, coarsely chopped
½ teaspoon turmeric
1 cup water

2 tablespoons vegetable oil
1½ pounds sirloin tips, sliced ¼ inch thick
1 tablespoon *prahok*, or more to taste (optional)
3½ cups water
3 tablespoons sugar
2 tablespoons fish sauce
4 teaspoons salt
½ cup tamarind juice
½ pound Chinese watercress or regular watercress, cut into 1-inch pieces
4 branches curry leaves *(sluk katrope)*, toasted (page 289)
Thinly sliced bird's eye chilies

TO MAKE THE PASTE: Blend all the ingredients in a blender until smooth, 2 to 3 minutes.

Heat the oil in a stockpot over medium-high heat. Add the paste, beef and *prahok*, if using, and sauté for 8 to 10 minutes, stirring constantly until the flavors are released. Add the water, sugar, fish sauce and salt and bring to a boil. Reduce the heat to low and simmer for 25 to 30 minutes, or until the meat is tender. Add the tamarind juice, watercress and toasted curry leaves and cook, stirring occasionally, for 5 minutes more.

Transfer the soup to a serving bowl and serve with rice, with chilies on the side.

SOUR SOUP WITH COCONUT MILK AND PINEAPPLE
Somlah Machou K'tih M'noa

SERVES 4

This full-bodied soup with a spice-infused coconut base features pork ribs and tart pineapple strips, with an aromatic lime-leaf accent. It's a fancy soup, and one that I like to experiment with, sometimes adding young winter melon and occasionally replacing the pork with duck. Although the *prahok* is optional, I urge you to try it in this recipe, where I think its pungency is essential.

PASTE

2 tablespoons thinly sliced lemongrass

2 dried New Mexico chilies, soaked, seeded and deveined

10 kaffir lime leaves, deveined

3 garlic cloves, coarsely chopped

2 pieces rhizome, each about 3 inches long, coarsely chopped

2 tablespoons coarsely chopped fresh cilantro stems

1 tablespoon peeled, coarsely chopped galangal

1 medium shallot, coarsely chopped

⅔ cup water

2 tablespoons vegetable oil

1 cup unsweetened coconut milk

⅓ cup *prahok* juice (optional)

1–1¼ pounds spareribs, separated and cut in half across the bone, or fresh ham, cut into 1-inch cubes

3 tablespoons fish sauce

1 tablespoon sugar

1 teaspoon salt

1 teaspoon shrimp paste

1 small slightly underripe pineapple (about 1 pound), peeled, cored, sliced ¼ inch thick and julienned

2 cups chicken broth

1 tablespoon fish powder (optional)

½ cup tamarind juice

5 kaffir lime leaves

TO MAKE THE PASTE: Blend all the ingredients in a blender until smooth, 2 to 3 minutes. Set aside.

Heat the oil in a large pot over medium-high heat. Add ½ cup of the coconut milk and cook, stirring, until the oil separates from the milk, 2 to 3 minutes. Add the lemongrass paste and cook, stirring often, until the flavors are released, another 2 to 3 minutes. Add the *prahok* juice (if using), along with the pork, fish sauce, sugar, salt and shrimp paste. Cook for 5 to 6 minutes to develop the flavors further.

Add the pineapple to the pot along with the remaining ½ cup coconut milk, chicken broth, fish powder (if using), and tamarind juice and simmer, partly covered, until the meat is tender, 45 to 50 minutes. Stir in the whole kaffir lime leaves and serve.

SOUR SOUP WITH TOMATO AND LOTUS
Somlah Machou Khmer

SERVES 4

3 cups chicken broth

2 stalks lemongrass, bottom halves only, smashed

¼ cup fish sauce

2 tablespoons sugar

2 teaspoons peeled, coarsely chopped galangal

2 teaspoons salt

¼ pineapple, peeled, cored, sliced ¼ inch thick and
    julienned

¼ pound lotus rootlets, cut into 2-inch lengths

1 medium tomato, cut into wedges

¾ pound catfish fillets, cut into 1-inch cubes

½ cup tamarind juice

3 tablespoons vegetable oil

10 garlic cloves, finely chopped

½ cup fresh basil leaves, coarsely chopped

⅓ cup coarsely chopped fresh *ma'am*, cilantro
    or mint

1 large egg, lightly beaten

Thinly sliced bird's eye chilies

This clear broth soup is a veritable feast for the senses. The sliced lotus stems are subtle in both flavor and texture, the pineapple and tomato provide zest and color and the basil and mint give off a heavenly aroma. Today, you can find this sour soup in most of the restaurants in Cambodia, where gourmets order it with plenty of fried garlic and lots of beaten egg. This soup is best served right away.

Put the chicken broth in a large stockpot and add the lemongrass, fish sauce, sugar, galangal and salt. Bring to a boil. Add the pineapple, lotus rootlets and tomato and return to a boil, then reduce the heat to low and simmer until the vegetables are soft, about 10 minutes. Gently stir in the catfish and tamarind juice and cook for another 10 minutes.

Meanwhile, heat the oil in a small pan over medium heat and fry the garlic until brown but not burned, 2 to 3 minutes; set aside.

When the fish is cooked, add the garlic, basil and *ma'am* or other herbs. Turn off the heat and add the egg, stirring it as it cooks.

Serve the soup piping hot with sliced bird's eye chilies.

LOBSTER SOUP WITH LIME
S'ngao B'kong

SERVES 4

6 cups chicken broth

3 garlic cloves, smashed

2 pounds freshwater lobster (with coral), shelled
  and deveined, or 1½ pounds jumbo shrimp,
  shelled and deveined

2 tablespoons fish sauce, plus more for serving

2 teaspoons sugar

1 teaspoon salt

½ scallion, sliced ¼ inch thick

Handful of fresh basil leaves, for garnish

3½ tablespoons fresh lime juice

Thinly sliced bird's eye chilies

The taste of lime juice and the rich flavor of lobster sparkle in this clear broth soup. But shrimp is also wonderful in this recipe; I like to split it deeply down the back, butterfly-style, and cut it into bite-sized pieces. The Cambodian way to eat Lobster Soup with Lime is to spoon some of the broth over rice with the lobster or shrimp pieces on the side — the remaining broth is to be drunk separately or not, according to taste.

Bring the broth and garlic to a boil in a large stockpot. Add the shellfish, fish sauce, sugar and salt and return to a boil. Reduce the heat to medium and cook at a high simmer until the lobsters are completely red or the shrimp are opaque (time will depend on their size, but figure about 5 minutes for a 1-pound lobster and 3 to 5 minutes for the shrimp); be careful not to overcook. Remove from the heat.

If using lobster, cut each one into 4 or 5 pieces (and release the pinkish orange coral from the head, pressing to break it open). Divide the lobster or shrimp and the broth among four large bowls and sprinkle with the scallion, basil and lime juice. Serve with lots of rice, more fish sauce and bird's eye chilies on the side.

WHITE FISH SOUP WITH YOUNG WINTER MELON
Somlah Machou Tralach

SERVES 4

4 cups chicken broth

2 teaspoons peeled, coarsely chopped galangal

2 garlic cloves, smashed

¾ pound young winter melon, peeled (or unpeeled zucchini or summer squash)

1 teaspoon *prahok* (optional)

½ cup tamarind juice

2 tablespoons fish sauce

2 teaspoons sugar

½ teaspoon salt

½ pound catfish fillets (or other firm white freshwater fish, such as tilapia), cut into 1-inch strips

⅓ cup coarsely chopped fresh *ma'am*, basil, cilantro or mint, for garnish

Thinly sliced red bell pepper, for garnish

This is my soul food. A simple broth cooked with freshwater fish, a green vegetable and some lively seasonings: this soup exemplifies Cambodia's healthful rural fare. You might want to try it in the summer because the young winter melon that it features, which resembles zucchini in taste and texture, is particularly valued as a cooling food — an important culinary contribution in a hot climate like ours. If you can find the herb *ma'am*, with its sharp flavor, like cilantro, in a Southeast Asian market, I think you'll agree that it's worth the effort; if you can't — and we never could when we lived in France — you can always use basil, cilantro or mint.

Bring the chicken broth, galangal and garlic to a boil in a large stockpot. Meanwhile, cut the winter melon crosswise into 1½-inch-thick slices and cut each slice into 8 wedges, as you would a pie.

When the broth is boiling, add the winter melon, return to a boil and reduce the heat to a simmer.

Put the *prahok* (if using) in a small bowl and add about 3 tablespoons of the hot broth, pressing down on the *prahok* with the back of a spoon to release its juices. Pour the flavored liquid — but not the solids — into the stockpot and add the tamarind juice, fish sauce, sugar and salt. Add the fish, stirring gently, and continue cooking until the winter melon is soft and the fish is opaque, 4 to 5 minutes.

Garnish with the *ma'am* or other herbs and sliced red pepper and serve with rice.

a blender until smooth, 2 to 3 minutes. Set aside.

In a stockpot, heat the oil. Add the coconut milk and cook over medium-high heat until the oil separates from the milk, about 2 minutes. Add the spice paste and cook for another 2 minutes, stirring constantly, until the aroma is released. Add the chicken and cook for 5 minutes, then stir in the chicken broth or water, sugar, fish sauce, *prahok* (if using) and salt. When the soup comes to a boil, reduce the heat to low, add the eggplant and tamarind juice and simmer gently for 10 minutes.

Pour into a soup tureen, garnish with the basil and serve with rice.

BEEF

CAMBODIANS VALUE BEEF VERY HIGHLY, but we don't eat a lot of it. It's my guess that this has something to do with our historical connection to India, where the cow is considered sacred and not a part of the diet. But there are other reasons, relating to agricultural patterns and regional husbandry, that account for the scarcity of cattle, and this in turn makes beef very costly.

One of the most common ways we eat beef, as you will see from the recipes, is in stir-fries, where we combine it with vegetables in lively and inventive ways in quantities small enough to be frugal but sufficiently large to be tasty and satisfying. We also commonly eat beef that has been marinated, in part because we have so many wonderful flavors we want to instill in our food, but also because our slim, free-range animals tend to be less than tender. Beef is also featured in some of the more elaborate dishes, in curries, stews and braises, where it shines.

I think one of my favorite beef recipes of all is Sweet Beef Stew. To me, it's like a Cambodian praise poem in honor of beef, a gastronomic expression of everything we value about it: the beautiful, rich color, tender texture and hearty flavor. When you can celebrate beef this fully, you don't have to do it so often.

MARINATED BEEF WITH LIME SAUCE

Loc Lac

SERVES 4

MARINADE

7 garlic cloves, finely chopped

2 tablespoons mushroom soy sauce

1 tablespoon sugar

1 teaspoon freshly ground pepper

1½ pounds flank steak or boneless sirloin, cut into
1½-inch squares

2 tablespoons vegetable oil

1 head green leaf lettuce, separated into leaves,
washed and drained

2 tablespoons fresh lime juice

1 teaspoon water

½ teaspoon freshly ground pepper

———————

TO MAKE THE MARINADE: Combine the garlic, soy sauce, sugar and pepper in a large bowl. Add the beef and stir to coat. Set aside for 30 minutes.

In a large skillet, heat the oil over high heat. Sauté the beef until medium-rare, 3 to 4 minutes. Arrange the lettuce leaves on a platter and place the beef cubes on top.

Combine the lime juice, water and pepper in a small bowl and serve with the beef as a dipping sauce.

My favorite part of this dish — besides its simplicity — is the aromatic flavor of the pepper. When we were in Cambodia recently, we saw *Loc Lac* on lots of restaurant menus, offered with slices of onion and tomato, french fries and even half a hard-boiled egg — all nice new touches. For a very simple but delightful meal, serve this dish with rice and a salad, using the dipping sauce for the meat but also as a splash of flavor over everything else.

GRILLED BEEF WITH DIPPING SAUCE
Saiko Ang Tuk Chralouark

SERVES 4

LEMONGRASS SAUCE

1½ teaspoons *prahok* juice (page 302)

1 garlic clove, pounded to a paste

½ stalk lemongrass, sliced as thin as possible and
   chopped

1 bird's eye chili, thinly sliced (seeded, if desired, for
   milder flavor)

2 tablespoons fresh lime juice

1 tablespoon fish sauce

1 teaspoon sugar

¼ teaspoon salt

½ English cucumber, thinly sliced

1 cup loosely packed fresh mint leaves

1 cup loosely packed fresh basil leaves

1¼ pounds top loin or sirloin tips, cut into
   2-inch squares

TO MAKE THE SAUCE: Mix all the ingredients in a small bowl, stirring well to dissolve the sugar.

Arrange rows of cucumber slices, mounds of the herb leaves and an individual bowl of dipping sauce on each plate.

Preheat the broiler and position a rack 4 inches from the heat. Lay the beef squares out on the broiler pan and place under the broiler. Cook, turning once, for 3 to 4 minutes per side for medium-rare, or to suit your preference for doneness. Remove and slice the meat across the grain into ⅛-inch-thick slices. Arrange on the plates and serve.

Lime juice is the dominant flavor in the dipping sauce used to enliven the tender slices of broiled beef in this dish, and it complements the accompanying fresh herbs and vegetables perfectly. Fish sauce and *prahok* are the sauce's more silent ingredients, but they give it its depth. Because I love the taste of *prahok*, I like to bring out the flavor of it even more by doubling the amount listed here. But for people who don't care for *prahok* or who don't have it on hand, Classic Dipping Sauce (see opposite) is an excellent alternative to the stronger Lemongrass Sauce. Feel free to add any additional fresh vegetables that you like: string beans, eggplant and cabbage are particularly good choices.

CLASSIC DIPPING SAUCE
Tuk Chralouark

SERVES 4

    ¾ cup fresh lime juice (3–4 limes)

    4 garlic cloves, pounded to a paste

    2 teaspoons salt

    1 teaspoon freshly ground pepper

Combine all the ingredients in a bowl, mixing well.

STIR-FRIED BEEF WITH CHINESE CELERY
Cha Saiko Nung Kinchai

SERVES 4

When I don't have any other ideas about what to make for supper, I can always make this dish; my husband, Ken, loves it. The combination of beef and celery has a wonderfully fresh taste to it, and the celery adds crunchiness. *Kinchai* is the Chinese name for celery, making the origin of this recipe clear, but the addition of sugar, garlic and fish sauce gives the stir-fry its distinctively Cambodian flavor.

¼ cup vegetable oil

6 garlic cloves, smashed

1 pound boneless sirloin, cut into strips 2 inches
    long, 1½ inches wide and ¼ inch thick

¾ pound Chinese celery or regular celery hearts,
    leaves included, sliced on the diagonal
    ½ inch thick

3½ tablespoons fish sauce

2 tablespoons sugar

1 teaspoon salt

1 pound tomatoes, cored and cut into bite-sized
    chunks

Heat the oil in a large skillet or wok over medium-high heat and stir-fry the garlic for 5 to 10 seconds, until browned but not burned. Add the beef and stir-fry for 2 minutes. Add the celery and cook for 2 minutes, then stir in the fish sauce, sugar and salt.

Carefully fold in the tomatoes and cook for 6 minutes: you want the beef to be cooked through, the celery to have some bite left and the tomatoes to retain some shape. Serve immediately with rice.

STIR-FRIED BEEF WITH PINEAPPLE
Cha Saiko Nung M'noa

SERVES 4

The acidic sweetness of the pineapple is a perfect complement to the moist and tender beef, and this stir-fry used to be a perennial favorite at our restaurant in France. Because we often couldn't get fresh pineapple, I was forced to use canned, which, to my surprise, turned out to be an excellent substitute.

5 tablespoons vegetable oil
1 tablespoon mushroom soy sauce
1¼ pounds boneless sirloin, cut into strips 2 inches long, 1½ inches wide and ¼ inch thick
2 garlic cloves, smashed
1 small pineapple (about 1 pound), peeled, cored, sliced ¼ inch thick and julienned, or 12 ounces canned pineapple slices, julienned
2 tablespoons fish sauce
2 teaspoons sugar
1 teaspoon cornstarch, dissolved in 1 tablespoon water (optional)
2 scallions, cut into 1½-inch pieces

Combine 2 tablespoons of the oil and the soy sauce in a shallow bowl and marinate the beef in this mixture for 10 minutes.

Heat the remaining 3 tablespoons oil in a large skillet or wok over medium-high heat and sauté the garlic until golden brown, 5 to 10 seconds. Add the beef, stirring well, then add the pineapple, fish sauce and sugar and stir-fry for 4 to 5 minutes.

If you want a thicker sauce, add the cornstarch-and-water paste to the pan, stirring well, and cook until the sauce has thickened, about 1 minute. Stir in the scallions and serve immediately with rice.

STIR-FRIED BEEF WITH TOMATOES
Saiko Cha Peng Pah

SERVES 4

3 tablespoons vegetable oil

2 garlic cloves, smashed

1 pound boneless sirloin, cut into strips 2 inches
    long, 1½ inches wide and ¼ inch thick

3 tablespoons fish sauce

1 tablespoon mushroom soy sauce

1 tablespoon sugar

2 medium slightly underripe tomatoes (about
    ¾ pound), cut into ½-inch-thick wedges

2 scallions, cut into 1½-inch pieces

This combination of tender beef and tart, not-quite-ripe tomatoes is the kind of stir-fry that used to be popular in the provinces of Cambodia and a dish you could find in any Chinese restaurant in any small town. It's very simple and cheery, with the red and green of the tomatoes and scallions, and it's also really tasty.

Heat the oil in a large skillet or wok over medium-high heat. Sauté the garlic until golden brown, 5 to 10 seconds. Add the beef, fish sauce, soy sauce and sugar, stirring well after each addition. Gently fold in the tomatoes and cook until they are heated through but not mushy, 3 to 4 minutes. Add the scallions, stirring well, and remove from the heat. Serve with rice.

STIR-FRIED BEEF WITH LEMONGRASS
Cha Saiko Kroeung

SERVES 4 TO 6

It is most unusual to find the normally straight-forward stir-fry being made with a spice paste, but here you have a perfect Indian-Chinese hybrid. The lemongrass in the paste has a strong, balmy presence, and the turmeric lends a yellow shade; at the royal palace, to make the dish fancier, chefs would add red chilies to the paste. Regal or not, the stir-fry is good with rice, a salad and some French bread.

PASTE

2 stalks lemongrass, thinly sliced
5 garlic cloves, coarsely chopped
1 large shallot, coarsely chopped
1½ teaspoons peeled, coarsely chopped galangal
6 kaffir lime leaves, deveined
2 tablespoons chopped fresh cilantro stems
½ teaspoon turmeric
2 dried New Mexico chilies, soaked, seeded and
    deveined, or 2 red bird's eye chilies, seeded and
    deveined (optional)
⅔ cup water

3 tablespoons vegetable oil
1¼ pounds boneless sirloin, cut into strips 2 inches
    long, 1½ inches wide and ¼ inch thick
3 tablespoons fish sauce
2 tablespoons sugar
½ teaspoon salt
1 large onion (about ¾ pound), sliced into
    ¼-inch-thick wedges
¼ red bell pepper, thinly sliced
4 scallions, split lengthwise and cut into
    2-inch pieces
½ cup peanuts, roasted and coarsely
    ground
Cilantro sprigs, for garnish

———

TO MAKE THE PASTE: Blend all the ingredients in a blender until smooth, 2 to 3 minutes.

Transfer the paste to a medium bowl, add the meat and mix well.

Heat the oil in a large skillet or wok over medium-high heat. Add the beef slices, stirring well, then add the fish sauce, sugar and salt and cook, stirring, until the sauce is bubbling, about 3 minutes. Add the onion and cook until soft and translucent, 3 to 4 minutes. Add the red pepper, scallions and 6 tablespoons of the peanuts. Cook, stirring, for another minute. Remove from the heat.

Sprinkle with the remaining 2 tablespoons peanuts and garnish with cilantro sprigs. Serve with rice.

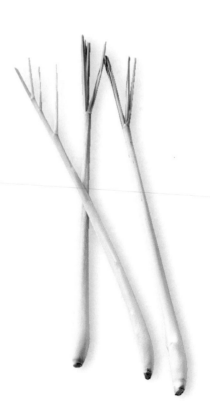

SPICY STIR-FRIED BEEF
Saiko Cha K'dao

SERVES 4

With its thin slices of light green cubanelle peppers and dark green jalapeños set against a turmeric-yellow sauce, this stir-fry makes a lovely meal. The sauce is especially flavorful, and you can stir in some chicken broth (up to ½ cup) just before serving to make it go further. Spicy Stir-Fried Beef is a specialty of the Battambang region in the northwest of Cambodia and a wonderful example of the inventiveness of rural cuisine. The fresh herb *mareh preuw*, holy basil, will remind Cambodians of home, but fresh sweet basil is a fine substitute.

¾ pound cubanelle peppers (about 3 large)
¼ pound jalapeño peppers (about 5)

PASTE

2 tablespoons thinly sliced lemongrass
2 large garlic cloves, coarsely chopped
1 medium shallot, coarsely chopped
2 teaspoons peeled, coarsely chopped galangal
½ teaspoon turmeric
½ cup water

¼ cup vegetable oil
1 pound boneless sirloin, cut into strips 2 inches
    long, 1½ inches wide and ¼ inch thick
1½ tablespoons sugar
1 tablespoon fish sauce
1 teaspoon salt
2 cups loosely packed fresh *mareh preuw* or regular
    basil leaves

Slice the cubanelle peppers very thinly lengthwise, removing the seeds and veins, then cut into 2-inch lengths. Slice the jalapeños very thinly lengthwise as well, removing the seeds (or retain them if you want to make the dish extra-hot).

TO MAKE THE PASTE: Blend all the ingredients in a blender until smooth, 2 to 3 minutes.

Heat the oil in a large skillet or wok over medium-high heat. Add the paste and cook until its aroma is released, about

1 minute. Stirring well as you go, add the beef, peppers, sugar, fish sauce and salt, and simmer for 3 to 4 minutes, until the meat is cooked through. Remove from the heat and add the basil leaves. Serve with rice.

STIR-FRIED BEEF WITH BITTER MELON
Cha Saiko Nung Mareh

SERVES 4

Bitter melon, with its quinine aftertaste, is usually a challenging flavor for non-Cambodians, but it is such an authentic Khmer flavor that I hesitate to strike it altogether from the culinary record. This recipe is an intriguing introduction to an exotic vegetable, and sugar and the heartiness of the meat balance its sharpness.

5 tablespoons vegetable oil
1 tablespoon mushroom soy sauce
1 pound sirloin tips, thinly sliced across the grain
1 firm bitter melon (about ¾ pound)
2 garlic cloves, smashed
2 tablespoons fish sauce
4 teaspoons sugar

Combine 2 tablespoons of the oil with the soy sauce in a medium bowl and marinate the beef in this mixture for 10 minutes.

Meanwhile, prepare the bitter melon: cut it lengthwise in half, scoop out the seeds and slice on an angle ¼ inch thick (you should have about 3 cups).

In a large skillet or wok, heat the remaining 3 tablespoons oil over medium-high heat and sauté the garlic until golden, 5 to 10 seconds. Stirring well after each addition, add the marinated meat, the bitter melon, fish sauce and sugar. Cook until the melon is soft but not mushy and its bitterness has mellowed a bit, 6 to 7 minutes. Serve with lots of rice.

BEEF WITH EGGPLANT IN COCONUT MILK
Keing Saiko

SERVES 4

PASTE

4 dried New Mexico chilies, soaked, seeded and
  deveined

1 stalk lemongrass, thinly sliced

5 garlic cloves, coarsely chopped

2 large shallots, coarsely chopped

2 teaspoons peeled, coarsely chopped galangal

8 kaffir lime leaves, deveined

¼ teaspoon turmeric

2 tablespoons chopped fresh cilantro stems

1½ cups water

¼ cup vegetable oil

2¼ cups unsweetened coconut milk

1 teaspoon shrimp paste

2 pounds flank steak or boneless sirloin, cut into
  strips 2 inches long, 1½ inches wide and ¼ inch
  thick

¼ cup fish sauce

¼ cup sugar

1 teaspoon salt

2 cups water

¼ pound pea eggplant, left whole, or Asian
  eggplant, cut into quarters

Fresh basil leaves, for garnish

Keing is the Thai word for anything cooked with coconut, and *saiko* in Khmer means beef, but it's the eggplant that distinguishes this full-bodied dish. When I was a girl, a vendor outside my school sold it on baguettes — a beef curry submarine — which I suppose is why, even to this day, I like to eat *Keing Saiko* with good French bread. Whether served as a main course with the traditional rice accompaniment or as an appetizer, this is essentially a stew, and like all stews, the longer it sits, the better it tastes.

TO MAKE THE PASTE: Blend all the ingredients in a blender until smooth, 2 to 3 minutes. Set aside.

Heat 3 tablespoons of the oil in a large pot over medium-high heat. Add 1 cup of the coconut milk and cook, stirring,

until the oil in the coconut milk separates out, 2 to 3 minutes. Stir in the spice paste and shrimp paste and cook until the flavors are released and the sauce is thickened and shiny, about 5 minutes.

Stir in the beef and cook for 5 to 6 minutes, until the meat has absorbed the flavor of the paste. Add the fish sauce, sugar, salt, the remaining 1¼ cups coconut milk and water and bring to a boil. Lower the heat to medium and simmer, stirring occasionally, for 30 to 40 minutes, or until the meat is tender.

Meanwhile, heat the remaining 1 tablespoon oil in a small skillet. Add the eggplant and sauté until soft, about 5 minutes.

Stir the eggplant into the stew and cook until heated through, 2 to 3 minutes.

Serve garnished with basil.

SWEET BEEF STEW
Khar Saiko Kroeung

SERVES 4

A *khar* is any sauce that has been reduced, and it is typically made with green coconut juice. This dish, which tastes a lot like a rich beef stew with carrots, is meant to be sweet, but in characteristic Cambodian fashion, salt provides a subtle balance. The use of ginger juice to marinate meat will probably be new to you, but it is very common in Cambodian cooking and produces a flavorful, tender result. For all the novelty of its ingredients and techniques, though, the result is a comfort food of the highest order.

2 pounds boneless top round or strip steak, cut into
   1½-inch cubes
½ cup peeled, thinly sliced ginger (about 2 ounces)

PASTE
3 dried New Mexico chilies, soaked, seeded and
   deveined
3 garlic cloves, coarsely chopped
1 large shallot, coarsely chopped
½ cup water

5 tablespoons vegetable oil
3 tablespoons sugar
2 tablespoons fish sauce
1 tablespoon mushroom soy sauce
1 teaspoon salt
1 teaspoon freshly ground pepper
1 cup chicken broth
1 cup green coconut juice
¼ cup tamarind juice
Cilantro sprigs, for garnish
Cucumber slices

Put the beef in a medium bowl. Grind the ginger slices with a mortar and pestle, adding them a few at a time until you have extracted most of the juice, or use a mini-chop to make a wet paste. Squeeze the juice from the fibers (you should have 1½ to 2 tablespoons) and stir it into the beef; discard the ginger solids. Let the beef marinate for at least 10 minutes.

MEANWHILE, MAKE THE PASTE: Blend all the ingredients in a blender until smooth, 2 to 3 minutes.

Heat the oil in a large pot over medium-high heat. Add the paste and cook, stirring occasionally, until the flavors are released, about 2 minutes. Stir in the beef, sugar, fish sauce, soy sauce, salt, pepper and broth. Bring to a boil, reduce the heat to low and simmer, partially covered, until the liquid is reduced by half, about 40 minutes.

Add the coconut and tamarind juices and cook for another 20 minutes. If the sauce is too thin at this point, increase the heat and reduce further; the sauce should be fairly thick.

Garnish with cilantro sprigs and serve with cucumber slices and rice.

BRAISED BEEF CURRY WITH PEANUTS
Saraman

SERVES 6 TO 8

With its combination of spices, coconut milk, peanuts and braised meat, this meal is rich and exotic indeed. *Saraman* is of obvious Indian origin and — as with most curries — the knowledge of its spice mixture was once jealously guarded by elderly women cooks. The dominant flavors here are cardamom and ginger, but each of the many other herbs and spices plays a significant role. The spice mixture freezes well, and there will be enough left over to make this dish two more times. On at least one of those other *Saraman* occasions, you might try substituting duck legs for the beef, as that combination is also splendid.

2½ pounds boneless top round, cut into 1½-inch cubes
½ cup peeled, thinly sliced ginger (about 2 ounces)

PASTE
3 tablespoons vegetable oil
4 dried New Mexico chilies, soaked, seeded, deveined and torn in half
2 teaspoons peeled, coarsely chopped galangal
7 garlic cloves, quartered
3 large shallots, cut into ¼-inch-thick slices
2 cinnamon sticks
4 whole star anise
20 cardamom seeds
1 whole Asian nutmeg, with mace attached
2 stalks lemongrass, thinly sliced
2½ cups water
¼ cup coarsely chopped fresh cilantro
½ teaspoon turmeric

¼ cup vegetable oil
4–4¾ cups unsweetened coconut milk
1½ teaspoons shrimp paste
5 tablespoons sugar
¼ cup fish sauce
¼ cup tamarind juice
1 teaspoon salt
1 cup peanuts, roasted
Thinly sliced bird's eye chilies

Put the beef in a medium bowl. Grind the ginger slices with a mortar and pestle, adding them a few at a time until you have extracted most of the juice, or use a mini-chop to make a wet paste. Squeeze the juice from the fibers (you should have 1½ to 2 tablespoons) and stir it into the beef; discard the ginger solids. Set the beef aside to marinate for at least 10 minutes.

MEANWHILE, MAKE THE PASTE: Heat the oil in a large skillet over medium-high heat. Add the chilies, galangal, garlic, shallots, cinnamon, star anise, cardamom, nutmeg and lemongrass and cook, stirring and shaking the pan, until golden brown, 6 to 7 minutes. Remove from the heat and cool slightly.

Scrape about half the cooked spices into a blender with the water and blend. Add the remaining cooked spices, the cilantro and turmeric and blend until very smooth, 4 to 5 minutes.

In a large pot, heat the oil over medium-high heat. Add 1½ cups of the coconut milk and let it come to a boil without stirring, cooking until the oil and milk separate, 4 to 5 minutes. Add ½ cup of the spice paste, the shrimp paste and marinated beef and cook, stirring occasionally, for about 15 minutes. (Freeze the leftover paste in two batches.)

Add another 2½ cups coconut milk, the sugar, fish sauce, tamarind juice, salt and peanuts. Stir well to distribute the ingredients evenly, reduce the heat to low and cook, covered, for 1¼ to 1½ hours, until the meat is very tender and the sauce is thickened. If it becomes too thick, add as much of the remaining ¾ cup coconut milk as needed.

Serve with rice or bread and lots of bird's eye chilies.

PORK

PORK IS THE MEAT MOST HEARTILY EMBRACED BY Cambodians. I suspect this is mostly due to the fact that the pig is the only animal we raise that has any significant amount of fat on it. (Until recently, rendered pork fat was our main source of oil for cooking.) There are all sorts of other factors having to do with the efficiency with which pigs convert grain into meat and their unmatched ability to live off whatever is available that explain their popularity, but the gustatory bottom line is that we love the way pork tastes.

In Cambodian cooking, pork is not only a main ingredient, but also a flavoring. For example, its broth serves as a rich backdrop against which to play off a wide variety of other flavors, as in Classic Noodle Soup, *K'tieu* (page 78). We also pair pork with an almost infinite variety of vegetables, and we use it to complement fruits, as in Pineapple Salad (page 235) or Pomelo Salad (page 236). While such combinations may initially appear novel to a Westerner, the Cambodian versions of barbecued ribs and seasoned sausage will strike a familiar chord and are truly splendid.

In the following recipes, I have routinely suggested using pork tenderloin because it is a familiar cut, easy to find and relatively lean, suiting the current American taste. From the Cambodian perspective, however, the fattier the pork, the better. In an Asian market, it is pork belly, with its baconlike layering of fat and meat, that is most highly valued; fat-marbled fresh ham is another favorite. I recommend that you try these cuts at least once or twice, perhaps in a rich ragout like Pork with Peanuts and Lilies or Spicy Sauced Pork, so that you have the opportunity to understand our aesthetic firsthand.

STIR-FRIED PORK WITH ONIONS

Cha Saik Chrouk Nung K'tum Barang

SERVES 4

3 tablespoons vegetable oil

1 pound pork tenderloin or fresh ham, cut into
   pieces 1½ inches long, 1½ inches wide and ¼
   inch thick

2 tablespoons fish sauce

2 teaspoons sugar

½ teaspoon white vinegar

1 large onion (about ¾ pound), cut into
   ½-inch-thick wedges

2 scallions, cut into 1½-inch pieces

Onions are common in Cambodian cuisine, and they taste wonderful with pork, as demonstrated by this simple stir-fry. Cambodians would tend to make this dish saltier, adding as much as 1½ teaspoons salt in addition to the fish sauce. Like all stir-fries, this one goes well with rice, and its simplicity achieves near elegance when accompanied by a green salad.

Heat the oil in a large skillet or wok over medium-high heat and add the meat. Stirring constantly, add the fish sauce, sugar and vinegar. Gently add the onion and stir-fry for 5 to 6 minutes, or until softened.

Add the scallions, stirring well, and remove from the heat. Serve with rice.

STIR-FRIED PORK WITH LONG BEANS
Cha Samdaik Trung

SERVES 4

3 tablespoons vegetable oil

4 garlic cloves, smashed

¾ pound pork tenderloin or fresh ham, cut into pieces 1½ inches long, 1½ inches wide and ¼ inch thick

3 tablespoons fish sauce

1½ tablespoons mushroom soy sauce

1½ tablespoons sugar

1 pound long beans or string beans, cut into 1½-inch pieces

¼ teaspoon freshly ground pepper

Heat the oil in a large skillet or wok over medium-high heat. Add the garlic and sauté for 5 to 10 seconds, until golden brown. Add the pork, stir in the fish sauce, soy sauce and sugar and cook for 2 to 3 minutes.

Add the beans and stir-fry for 5 to 6 minutes, until the meat is fully cooked. Add the pepper, stir well and serve.

Stir-fried pork and long beans is a delightful combination: fresh-tasting, filling and flavorful. Bunches of long beans are easy to find in Asian markets. They are perfect for stir-fries because they stay so firm and crunchy when they cook, and there's an almost meaty richness to them. String beans will taste just fine if you need to make a substitution, but you really should try the long beans.

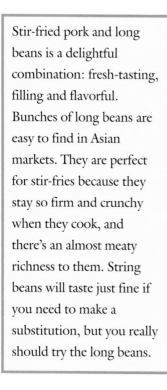

STIR-FRIED PORK WITH BEAN SPROUTS
Cha Samdaik Bandos

SERVES 4

3 tablespoons vegetable oil

4 garlic cloves, smashed

½ pound pork tenderloin or fresh ham, cut into
   pieces 1½ inches long, 1½ inches wide and
   ¼ inch thick

½ pound pressed bean curd or spiced dry tofu,
   cut into ¼-inch-thick slices

3 tablespoons fish sauce

1 tablespoon mushroom soy sauce

2 tablespoons sugar

½–¾ pound mung bean sprouts, to taste

½ pound Chinese chives or scallions, cut into
   2-inch pieces

¼ teaspoon freshly ground pepper

This pork stir-fry is a tasty, inexpensive meal and a good way to enjoy mung bean sprouts. You can easily substitute chicken for the pork, or, for something a little richer, try duck breast with the skin on. A vegetarian version of this recipe is easy to make: just add 4 to 6 ounces of pressed bean curd in place of the meat.

Heat the oil in a large skillet or wok over medium-high heat. Add the garlic and sauté until golden brown, 5 to 10 seconds. Stirring well after each addition, add the pork, bean curd or spiced tofu, fish sauce, soy sauce and sugar. Add the bean sprouts, folding in gently, and cook for 4 to 5 minutes, until the pork is done.

Add the chives or scallions and pepper and stir-fry for another minute, until heated through. Serve immediately.

EGGPLANT AND PORK STIR-FRY
Cha Traop Dot

SERVES 4

3 large eggplant (about 4 pounds)
¼ cup vegetable oil
5 garlic cloves, smashed and coarsely chopped
¾ pound ground pork
¾ pound shrimp, shelled, deveined and
   finely chopped
¼ cup fish sauce
1½ tablespoons sugar
½ teaspoon freshly ground pepper
3 scallions, thinly sliced

———————

Preheat the oven to 350°F.

Prick the eggplant with a fork, put it on a baking sheet and bake for 45 minutes, or until soft. Allow to cool slightly, then peel and discard the skins and mash the flesh with a fork until smooth. Set aside.

Heat the oil in a large skillet over medium-high heat. Add the garlic and sauté until golden brown, about 10 seconds. Stir in the pork and shrimp, breaking up any clumps, then add the fish sauce, sugar and pepper. When well mixed, add the eggplant and continue stir-frying until it is warmed through, about 3 minutes. Add the scallions, stir well, remove from the heat and serve.

With relatively few ingredients, this pork and eggplant stir-fry delivers an enormous amount of flavor: sweet, smoky and rich. In Cambodia, the eggplant would be painstakingly cooked over a charcoal fire before being stir-fried with the meat, but baking it in the oven simplifies the process considerably. I like the combination of pork and shrimp, but pork by itself is also good, or you can substitute ¾ pound chicken for the shrimp if fat is a concern.

STIR-FRIED GREEN SQUASH WITH PORK
Cha Clohk Nung Saik Chrouk

SERVES 4

3 tablespoons vegetable oil

3 garlic cloves, smashed

½ pound ground pork

1½ tablespoons fish sauce

1 teaspoon sugar

1½ pounds Asian squash, peeled (or unpeeled zucchini), julienned

1 large egg, lightly beaten

1 scallion, sliced ¼ inch thick

½ teaspoon freshly ground pepper

Made with pork, squash and egg, this stir-fry boasts such a range of tastes and textures that you need little more than rice to complete the meal. If you can find it, Asian squash is a nice addition. It looks like a large summer squash but is pale green. You can also use zucchini; allow about 2 minutes less time for cooking. By simply skipping the pork and adding a couple of extra eggs, you can make this dish meatless, which is the way my father always liked it.

Heat the oil in a large skillet or wok over medium-high heat and sauté the garlic until golden brown, 5 to 10 seconds. Add the pork, fish sauce, sugar and squash and cook, stirring to break up the pork, for 3 minutes for zucchini or 5 minutes for Asian squash, or until the vegetables are tender.

Add the egg and cook, stirring, until it is firm. Remove from the heat, sprinkle with the scallion and pepper, stir well and serve.

STIR-FRIED BUTTERCUP SQUASH WITH PORK
Cha L'poh

SERVES 4

Though it uses just a few ingredients, this gem of a stir-fry is complex in taste, with the sweetness of squash balancing the slightly salty pork. I was excited to find buttercup squash in this country — it's exactly the kind we have in Cambodia.

3 tablespoons vegetable oil

3 garlic cloves, smashed

½ pound pork tenderloin or fresh ham, cut into pieces 1½ inches long, 1½ inches wide and ¼ inch thick

2 tablespoons fish sauce

1 teaspoon sugar

1¼ pounds buttercup squash, peeled, seeds scooped out, julienned

2 scallions, cut into 1½ inch pieces

¼ teaspoon freshly ground pepper

Heat the oil in a large skillet or wok over medium-high heat and sauté the garlic until golden brown, 5 to 10 seconds. Add the pork, stirring well, then add the fish sauce and sugar. Fold in the squash gently and stir-fry until it is cooked through but still slightly crunchy, 4 to 5 minutes (or longer if you prefer a softer texture).

Add the scallions and pepper and stir well. Serve hot with rice.

STIR-FRIED PORK WITH TOFU AND CHIVE BLOSSOMS
Cha P'ka Kuchai

SERVES 4

Chive blossoms, which you can find in Asian markets in hanks about a foot long, transform this simple stir-fry into a thing of beauty. The taste of the chive blossoms is very strong when they are fresh, but the flavor mellows in the nicest way as they cook. A vegetarian version of this dish can be made easily by simply omitting the pork and substituting 1 teaspoon of salt for the fish sauce.

¼ cup vegetable oil

4 garlic cloves, smashed

¾ pound pork tenderloin or fresh ham, cut into pieces 1½ inches long, 1½ inches wide and ¼ inch thick

½ pound spiced dry tofu or pressed bean curd, cut into ¼-inch cubes

¼ cup fish sauce

2 tablespoons sugar

¾–1 pound chive blossoms and stems or scallions, cut into 2-inch pieces

½ teaspoon freshly ground pepper

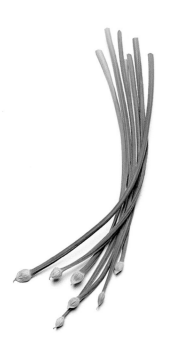

Heat the oil in a large skillet or wok over medium-high heat. Add the garlic and sauté for 5 to 10 seconds, or until golden brown. Add the pork and stir-fry for 2 to 3 minutes.

Stirring gently after each addition, add the tofu or bean curd, fish sauce, sugar and chives or scallions and cook for about 5 minutes, until the meat is thoroughly cooked but the chives are still crisp. Toss with the pepper and serve.

SPICY SAUCED PORK
Kapik Khing

SERVES 4

PASTE

2 dried New Mexico chilies, soaked, seeded and
    deveined
1 stalk lemongrass, thinly sliced
3 garlic cloves, coarsely chopped
1 large shallot, coarsely chopped
4 kaffir lime leaves, deveined
2 bird's eye chilies
1 teaspoon shrimp paste
2 pieces rhizomes, each 2 inches long
¼ teaspoon turmeric
¼ cup coarsely chopped fresh cilantro stems
1 cup water

3 tablespoons vegetable oil
2½ pounds pork belly (skin on), fresh ham or pork
    tenderloin, cut into pieces 1½ inches long,
    1½ inches wide and ¼ inch thick
5 tablespoons sugar
1 tablespoon fish sauce
1¼ teaspoons salt
3 tablespoons fish powder

My husband, Ken, always appreciates this pork dish with its richly spiced sauce, and I like to serve it to him with rice or slices of good bread and a simple salad. You might want to try the dish as an appetizer by spreading it over a piece of Crispy Rice (page 203), topping that with a thin slice of cucumber and garnishing with a sprig of cilantro — it's very good that way.

TO MAKE THE PASTE: Blend all the ingredients in a blender until smooth, 2 to 3 minutes. Set aside.

Heat the oil in a large skillet over medium-high heat. Sauté the pork, stirring, for about 5 minutes. Stir in the paste, sugar, fish sauce and salt. Reduce the heat to low and cook, stirring occasionally, until the liquid has nearly evaporated and the pork is tender, 20 to 30 minutes. Add the fish powder and cook for another 2 minutes. Serve hot.

PORK WITH PINEAPPLE
Keing D'ananas

SERVES 4 TO 8

2 pounds spareribs or baby back ribs, or 1½ pounds
   fresh ham

PASTE

3 dried New Mexico chilies, soaked, seeded and
   deveined
1 stalk lemongrass, thinly sliced
4 garlic cloves, coarsely chopped
2 large shallots, coarsely chopped
10 kaffir lime leaves, deveined
2 tablespoons chopped fresh cilantro stems
1 tablespoon peeled, coarsely chopped galangal
¼ teaspoon turmeric
1 cup water

¼ cup vegetable oil
2½ cups unsweetened coconut milk
2 teaspoons shrimp paste
¼ cup sugar
2 tablespoons fish sauce
2 teaspoons salt
2 cups water
1 slightly underripe small pineapple
   (about 1 pound), peeled, cored and julienned
¼ cup fish powder
5 kaffir lime leaves, deveined
1 tablespoon fresh lime juice
Fresh basil leaves, for garnish

I love the strong, distinctive flavor combination of pineapple and smoked fish in this stew. When I was young, it was the first dish with coconut milk that I wanted to learn to cook. It's very rich fare — which is why I've suggested such a wide range for the number of servings — but the acidity of the still-green pineapple and the lime juice keeps it lively. You may also want to ask your butcher to cut the ribs into pieces for you.

If using ribs, cut them into 1½-inch pieces across the bone, then cut between the bones to create bite-sized pieces.

If using ham, cut into pieces 2 inches long by 1½ inches wide and ½ inch thick.

TO MAKE THE PASTE: Blend all the ingredients in a blender until smooth, 2 to 3 minutes. Set aside.

Heat the oil in a large skillet over medium-high heat. Add 1 cup of the coconut milk and cook, stirring constantly, until the oil separates from the milk, 2 to 3 minutes. Add the spice paste and shrimp paste and cook, stirring occasionally, until the aroma of the spices is fully developed, about 5 minutes.

Stir in the pork, sugar, fish sauce and salt and cook for about 5 minutes. Add the water and the remaining 1½ cups coconut milk and bring to a boil. Reduce the heat to low, add the pineapple and simmer for 10 more minutes. Add the fish powder and kaffir lime leaves and cook until the pork is tender, 5 to 10 minutes more. Remove from the heat.

Stir in the lime juice, garnish with basil leaves and serve with rice.

PORK WITH PEANUTS AND LILIES
Hong Chrouk

SERVES 4

¼ cup fish sauce

2 tablespoons soy sauce

1 tablespoon salt

1 teaspoon freshly ground pepper

2 pounds pork belly, fresh ham or pork tenderloin,
    cut into 2-inch squares

2 tablespoons vegetable oil

3 garlic cloves, smashed

⅔ cup sugar

5 cups water

2 tablespoons mushroom soy sauce

4 whole star anise or 1 teaspoon ground anise

½ cup peanuts, roasted

30–35 dried lilies (about 1 ounce), soaked for
    10–15 minutes in warm water, drained and
    knotted (page 289)

Cilantro sprigs, for garnish

In this very sophisticated ragout, fried garlic, caramelized sugar, roasted peanuts and rich pork come together to produce a symphony of flavors. Because of the sauce's sweetness, the dish pairs perfectly with salty foods like Pickled Bean Sprouts (page 253) and Cambodian Cabbage Salad (page 230), which extend the gastronomic performance even further. This is a meal for savoring, so I try to make it when I have plenty of time. Rice is almost *de rigueur* here, as a support for all the other tastes and textures.

In a large bowl, combine the fish sauce, soy sauce, 2 teaspoons of the salt and the pepper. Add the pork, stir well and set aside to marinate for 30 minutes.

Heat the oil in a large deep skillet over medium-high heat and sauté the garlic until golden brown, 5 to 10 seconds. Lower the heat to medium, add the sugar and stir constantly as it liquifies, browns and froths, 3 to 4 minutes.

When the caramel is dark brown, stir in the pork and cook for 5 minutes. Add the water, bring to a boil and skim off any fat. Stir in the soy sauce, the remaining teaspoon salt, star anise and peanuts. Lower the heat and simmer, partially covered, for 30 minutes. Add the lilies and simmer for 20 to 30 minutes more, or until the pork is tender. Put in a large serving bowl and garnish with cilantro.

PORK WITH DIPPING SAUCE
Saik Chrouk Chralouark

SERVES 4

1¼ pounds pork tenderloin, pork belly or fresh
    ham, cut into 1½-inch cubes
3 ¼-inch-thick slices peeled galangal
3 garlic cloves, smashed and finely chopped
1 medium shallot, finely chopped
½ cup peanuts, roasted and coarsely ground
6 tablespoons fish sauce
3 tablespoons sugar
2 tablespoons white vinegar
Thinly sliced bird's eye chilies, for garnish
1 large head green leaf lettuce, separated into leaves,
    washed and dried
1 cup loosely packed fresh mint leaves
1 cup loosely packed fresh basil leaves
½ pound mung bean sprouts
½ English cucumber, cut lengthwise in half and
    thinly sliced

For this handsome, healthful dish, basil, mint and mung bean sprouts and slices of cucumber and pork are laid out in a most inviting way. The fun comes when you start putting it all together, wrapping everything up in lettuce leaves and dipping them in the zesty sauce, with its masterly blending of sweet, salty and acidic flavors. You can eat this dish with rice as a whole meal, or by itself. See the photograph on page 143.

Bring a large pot of water to a boil. Add the pork, return the water to a boil and cook, partially covered, until the meat is tender, about 25 minutes.

While the pork is cooking, impale the galangal slices on the tines of a fork and grill directly over a gas flame, or place them in a small heavy skillet and cook for 2 to 3 minutes, turning, until lightly browned.

Pound the galangal, garlic and shallot with a mortar and pestle or grind in a mini-chop to a paste, adding a couple of tablespoons of the ground peanuts if necessary to make it smoother. Transfer this paste to a bowl and add the fish sauce, sugar, vinegar and the rest of the peanuts. Stir well to dissolve the sugar; the sauce will be thick. Divide among four small bowls and sprinkle the chilies over each, as desired.

Drain the pork and allow to cool. Cut into $\frac{1}{8}$-inch-thick slices.

Arrange the lettuce, herbs, sprouts, sliced cucumbers and sliced pork in separate bowls or on a platter. Serve with small bowls of dipping sauce. To eat, put a little of each item on the platter in the center of a lettuce leaf, wrap and dip into the sauce.

STUFFED CABBAGE WITH LEMONGRASS AND CHILIES
Spey Kadop Nyuot Kroeung

SERVES 4

2 pounds green cabbage, tough outer leaves
 removed, cored

PASTE

1½ dried New Mexico chilies, soaked, seeded
 and deveined
½ stalk lemongrass, thinly sliced
2 kaffir lime leaves, deveined
2 garlic cloves, coarsely chopped
1 medium shallot, coarsely chopped
1 tablespoon coarsely chopped fresh cilantro
1 teaspoon peeled, coarsely chopped galangal
1 teaspoon shrimp paste
½ cup water

1 pound ground pork
1 large egg, lightly beaten
3 tablespoons unsweetened coconut milk
1½ tablespoons sugar
1 teaspoon salt
1 small bird's eye chili, seeded (or not, depending on
 your heat tolerance) and finely chopped
½ cup chicken broth
Vegetable oil

When we lived in Yugoslavia, we couldn't get any of the ingredients for Cambodian food and, during the wintertime, cabbage and potatoes were the only available produce. Because Cambodians make recipes such as this one, the many stuffed cabbage dishes of the Serbs seemed familiar to us and, therefore, comforting. The only real difference between Serbian and Cambodian stuffed cabbage is in the seasonings: the balmy fragrance of the lemongrass and the spiciness of the chilies make this dish distinctively Khmer. It can be baked in the oven or cooked on top of the stove.

Bring a large pot of water to a boil. Place the cabbage in the boiling water, bring the water back to a boil and blanch the cabbage for about 15 minutes, until the leaves are tender. Remove the cabbage and set aside to cool.

TO MAKE THE PASTE: Blend all the ingredients in a blender until smooth, 2 to 3 minutes.

Put the ground pork in a medium bowl and add ½ cup of the spice paste, leaving the rest in the blender. Mix thoroughly, then add the egg, coconut milk, sugar, salt and chili and mix well.

If you plan to bake the stuffed cabbage, preheat the oven to 375°F.

Carefully remove about 20 of the leaves from the cooled cabbage, keeping them whole (reserve any leftover cabbage for another use, such as Cambodian Cabbage Salad, page 230, or Mixed Vegetable Pickles, page 256). Cut each leaf in half lengthwise and cut away the center vein where it is too thick to fold easily. Place a heaping tablespoon of the pork mixture in the center of each leaf, folding in the sides first and then the top and bottom to make a small packet about 3 inches by 2 inches. You should be able to make 18 to 20 packets.

Add the chicken broth to the leftover paste in the blender, swirling to blend.

TO BAKE THE PACKETS: Arrange the stuffed cabbage seam side down in a 13-by-9-inch baking pan; if necessary, make two layers. Pour the broth-paste mixture over the top of the cabbage. Drizzle with 1 to 2 tablespoons oil and bake for 25 to 30 minutes, basting occasionally. To check for doneness, press down on the cabbage packets: if firm, they are fully cooked.

TO COOK THE PACKETS ON THE STOVE-TOP: Heat ¼ cup oil in a large, deep skillet over medium heat. Add the stuffed cabbage, pour the broth-paste mixture over it, lower the heat slightly and cook, turning the packets occasionally, until they are nicely browned and firm to the touch, 20 to 25 minutes. Serve immediately.

BRAISED TOMATOES STUFFED WITH PORK
Peng Pah Khmer

SERVES 4

8 slightly underripe, firm tomatoes (3½–4 pounds)
1¼ pounds ground pork
1 large egg, lightly beaten
2–3 scallions, white parts only, very thinly sliced
2 tablespoons chopped fresh cilantro stems
2 tablespoons sugar
1 tablespoon mushroom soy sauce, plus more for
    serving
2 teaspoons salt
½ teaspoon freshly ground pepper
¼ cup vegetable oil
4 garlic cloves, smashed and coarsely chopped
Cilantro sprigs, for garnish

Slightly underripe tomatoes are best for this dish. Their acidity is a perfect contrast for the richness of the pork, and braising brings out their flavor even more. The idea of stuffed tomatoes is definitely urban and upper-class and shows a strong French influence. Not surprisingly, then, French bread and a green salad make perfect accompaniments.

Cut off the top ½ inch of the tomatoes and spoon out the insides; reserve the tomato meat. Turn the tomatoes upside down on paper towels to drain briefly.

Meanwhile, mix together the pork, egg, scallions, cilantro, sugar, soy sauce, salt and pepper in a medium bowl. Chop the reserved tomato meat and add ⅓ cup of it to the pork.

Stuff the tomatoes with the meat mixture.

Heat the oil in a large skillet over medium-high heat and sauté the garlic until brown but not burned, 5 to 10 seconds. Remove the garlic and set aside.

Add the stuffed tomatoes, cut sides down, adjust the heat to low and cook, partially covered, for 25 minutes. Turn so the cut sides are up and cook until the meat is done throughout, about 25 minutes more.

Serve garnished with sprigs of cilantro and the fried garlic, with additional mushroom soy sauce on the side.

GRILLED MARINATED PORK RIBS
Ch'ang Chumnee Ang

SERVES 4

The experience of eating richly seasoned, crisply grilled pork ribs transcends any differences between East and West, and I think you'll find Cambodian-style ribs to be a great addition to the world's repertoire. At home, we always served ribs as one of several dishes for dinner, but since leaving Cambodia, my family and I are more likely to eat them with rice and some pickles (Mixed Vegetable Pickles, page 256, are my favorites) and call that a meal. You can adjust the amount of ribs in this recipe according to whether you want them as a side dish or as a centerpiece. You can always serve them as appetizers, as well. Be sure to leave plenty of time for marinating.

5 garlic cloves, smashed and coarsely chopped
3 tablespoons mushroom soy sauce
2 tablespoons sugar
1½ teaspoons salt
½ teaspoon freshly ground pepper
2½ pounds spareribs or baby back ribs
    (2–3 ribs per person), separated

Mix the garlic, soy sauce, sugar, salt and pepper together in a large bowl. Add the meat to the bowl, turning the ribs to coat well with the marinade, and allow to sit for at least 1 hour at room temperature or as long as overnight in the refrigerator.

Preheat the grill or broiler, positioning a rack about 6 inches from the heat. Grill the ribs until well browned and cooked through, 10 to 12 minutes per side. Serve immediately.

CAMBODIAN SAUSAGE
Saik Krok Khmer

SERVES 4

When I was growing up, we considered this richly seasoned sausage a fancy dish for guests, and whenever my parents had a party, the neighborhood would be filled with the enticing smell of it cooking over charcoal. I always loved the way the sausage looked, too: a giant coil lashed between bamboo splints. Even today, I am thrilled when I see it being served as part of a larger meal (which is the traditional way), as a simple dinner with rice or as an appetizer, with pickles and some good bread. If you don't have the equipment or time to make the sausage in casings, you can make patties instead. The mung beans should be soaked at least several hours or overnight, so plan ahead.

PASTE

½ stalk lemongrass, thinly sliced

1½ tablespoons chopped fresh cilantro stems

3 garlic cloves, coarsely chopped

1 large shallot, coarsely chopped

6 kaffir lime leaves, deveined

1 teaspoon peeled, coarsely chopped galangal

1 piece rhizome, about 3½ inches long

1 dried New Mexico chili, soaked, seeded and deveined

4 bird's eye chilies

½ cup water (omit if making sausage patties)

2 tablespoons unsweetened coconut milk (6 tablespoons if making sausage patties)

½ cup dried split mung beans, soaked for several hours or, preferably, overnight, drained

½ cup peanuts, roasted and coarsely ground

1½ pounds ground pork

3 tablespoons sugar

2 teaspoons salt

1 large egg, lightly beaten

1–2 tablespoons unsweetened coconut milk, if necessary

Sausage casings, soaked (optional)

Vegetable oil

TO MAKE THE PASTE: Blend all the ingredients in a blender until smooth, 2 to 3 minutes. Set aside.

Using a mortar and pestle or a mini-chop, coarsely grind the soaked mung beans and peanuts together. In a large bowl, combine the paste, peanut–mung bean mixture, pork, sugar, salt and egg and stir until thoroughly blended; if the mixture is too dry, add a tablespoon or two of coconut milk.

TO MAKE SAUSAGES IN CASINGS: Drain the sausage casings and rub them with 2 tablespoons oil. Using a sausage-making machine or a funnel and a chopstick, stuff the casings with the sausage mixture, preferably making one long sausage.

Preheat the grill or broiler, positioning a rack about 6 inches from the heat. Coil the sausage loosely on the grill, piercing the casing lightly in several places with a knife. Or, if using the broiler, spread 2 tablespoons oil in the bottom of the broiler pan, coil the sausage in the pan and pierce the casing. Grill or broil for 9 or 10 minutes per side, until cooked through.

Transfer the sausage to a platter. Slice the sausage coil on the diagonal, about 1½ inches thick, and serve with rice or bread and any kind of pickles.

TO MAKE SAUSAGE PATTIES: Shape 3 to 4 tablespoons of the sausage mixture into patties about ½ inch thick. Heat 1 tablespoon oil in a nonstick skillet over medium-high heat. Fry the sausage patties, turning once, until cooked through, 15 to 20 minutes.

PORK OMELET
Pong Mouan Snol

SERVES 4

2 tablespoons plus 1 teaspoon vegetable oil
½ pound ground pork
1 small onion, thinly sliced lengthwise
2 tablespoons preserved cabbage
1 tablespoon sugar
½ teaspoon salt
½ teaspoon freshly ground pepper
1 tablespoon plus 1 teaspoon mushroom soy sauce
6 large eggs
2 tablespoons thinly sliced scallion
Cilantro sprigs, for garnish

Filled with pork, scallions and preserved cabbage, this omelet is a favorite at my house. Its sweet and salty flavors are highlighted by the richness of the soy sauce and the aromatic pepper. Traditionally, we eat this dish with other entrees and rice; if you want to serve it as a meal by itself, you might want to increase the amounts by half. Some sliced tomatoes on the side are a nice addition.

Heat 2 tablespoons of the oil in a large skillet over medium-high heat. Add the pork, onion and preserved cabbage, stirring well to break apart the clumps of meat. Add the sugar, salt, pepper and 1 tablespoon of the soy sauce and cook for about 5 minutes, until the pork is no longer pink. Remove from the heat and set aside.

Beat the eggs lightly with the remaining 1 teaspoon soy sauce in a medium bowl. Heat a very large (at least 12-inch) nonstick skillet over medium-high heat and add the remaining 1 teaspoon oil; swirl the oil in the skillet to coat bottom lightly and pour off any excess. Add the eggs, tilting to distribute thinly and evenly over the bottom and halfway up the sides.

Spread the pork mixture over one side of the eggs and sprinkle with the scallions. Cook for 2 minutes, or until the eggs are nearly set. Fold over the omelet and cook until it is sealed, about 2 minutes more. Garnish with cilantro sprigs.

FISH AND SHELLFISH

A MAJOR FEATURE OF CAMBODIA'S NATURAL bounty is its incredible reserve of freshwater fish, the largest in the world. In the Tonle Sap Lake, particularly during the rainy season, live millions of catfish, elephant fish, mudfish, gray featherback fish, freshwater lobsters, shrimp, clams, mussels and eels. This abundance has shaped much of the basic framework of Cambodian cuisine.

If you could find a Khmer meal without fish as one of the entrees—and that's a big "if"—fish sauce, *prahok,* dried shrimp and smoked fish would still be mixed in. And then there are the special treats, like the tiny salted freshwater clams cooked by the midday sun that you eat as a snack, cracking open the shells with your teeth, dipping the meat into fish sauce with tamarind or green mangoes and chilies. Unlike Americans, who can be cautious about *fruits de mer,* Cambodians enthusiastically embrace fish-eating as a way of life.

I usually recommend freshwater fish for the recipes that follow because that's what I know and love best, but other firm white fish, such as sole or snapper, are also fine. Stir-fried and deep-fried, grilled and steamed, sautéed and curried, these fish dishes are a delectable adventure.

GINGER CATFISH
Trey Cha K'nyei

SERVES 4

5 tablespoons vegetable oil

2 cups peeled, julienned ginger (about ½ pound)

1½ pounds catfish fillets, sliced crosswise into
    ¼-inch-wide strips

3½ tablespoons sugar

2 tablespoons mushroom soy sauce

2 tablespoons fish sauce

1 teaspoon salt

1 large Spanish onion, thinly sliced

¼ red bell pepper, julienned

½ bunch scallions, cut diagonally into 2-inch pieces

———

Heat the oil in a large skillet over medium-high heat. Add the ginger and cook, stirring, until brown and crisp, about 7 minutes. Add the fish, stir gently until thoroughly mixed with the ginger and cook for about 3 minutes. Add the sugar, soy sauce, fish sauce and salt and stir well. Stir in the onion and cook for another 3 to 4 minutes. Add the red pepper and scallions and cook for another 2 minutes, then serve.

I am particularly fond of this stir-fry because of the hot, peppery taste and penetrating aroma that comes from using so much ginger, and I find that people who have never had it before fall in love with it for the same reason. Of course, if you like a milder flavor, feel free to use less ginger; just be careful not to make it too mild, or the dish will be bland. In Cambodia, we believe that ginger has medicinal qualities and that it heats up the head and the whole system to make you feel better. With this in mind, you might want to try Ginger Catfish the next time you have a cold.

GRILLED FISH
Trey Ang

SERVES 4

The combination of sweet and sour in this simple recipe for grilled fish with mango relish is typically Cambodian, and the overall effect is clean and fresh-tasting. You want the mango to be underripe, because the greener it is, the more sour, and you may have to go to an Asian market to find one. While you're there, you might also want to see if you can find frozen mudfish, which is the authentic fish for this dish and delicious, despite its name.

1–1½ pounds firm white freshwater fish fillets, such as catfish or tilapia, or 1 whole cleaned mudfish (about 2½ pounds)
1 large green mango
About 1 cup fish sauce, plus more for serving
About 1½ teaspoons sugar
2 garlic cloves, smashed and finely chopped
Thinly sliced bird's eye chilies

Preheat the broiler, positioning the rack 6 inches from the heat. Place the fish fillets or whole fish in a broiler pan and place under the broiler. Broil for 8 to 15 minutes (figure on 10 minutes of cooking time per inch of thickness of the fish), turning once, until nicely browned.

Meanwhile, peel the mango and cut the fruit away from the seed. Cut the flesh into julienne strips. Measure the mango strips and for every ½ cup, add ⅓ cup fish sauce and ½ teaspoon sugar. Add the garlic and stir well.

Serve the fish with the mango mixture, sliced chilies and additional fish sauce.

PAN-SEARED FISH WITH PORK AND SOYBEANS
Chien Chuoan

SERVES 4

This is the first Khmer dish I wanted to prepare myself, and I tried it only after I got married. I was particularly interested in learning to make the sauce that goes with the seared fish because I was intrigued by its combination of acidity and sweetness and the salty taste of the soybeans, a Chinese touch. Even now the blending of flavors continues to tempt me.

1 cup plus 2 tablespoons vegetable oil
1½–2 pounds catfish or sole fillets, cut crosswise in half
3 garlic cloves, smashed
¼ pound ginger, peeled and julienned (about 1 cup)
¼ pound ground pork
3 tablespoons sugar
2 tablespoons salted soybeans
2 teaspoons mushroom soy sauce
2½ tablespoons fish sauce
1 tablespoon white vinegar
⅔ cup water
2 scallions, sliced on the diagonal into 2-inch pieces
Julienned red bell pepper, for garnish
Cilantro sprigs, for garnish

Heat the 1 cup oil in a large skillet or wok over medium-high heat. When the oil is hot, add as many fillet halves as will fit comfortably in the pan without crowding. Pressing down on the middle of the pieces occasionally to ensure even cooking, fry the fish until golden brown, about 7 minutes per side. Remove from the pan with a slotted spoon and drain on paper towels. Cook the remaining pieces in the same fashion. Discard the oil.

Heat the remaining 2 tablespoons oil in the skillet or wok over medium-high heat and sauté the garlic until golden brown, 5 to 10 seconds. Add the ginger and cook, stirring occasionally, for 5 minutes. Add the pork and cook, stirring to break up the clumps, until the meat loses its red color, about 2 minutes. Stirring as you go, add the sugar, salted soybeans, soy sauce, fish sauce, vinegar and water and cook for about 4 minutes more, until the liquid has slightly reduced. Stir in the scallions and cook for 1 minute.

Return the fish to the pan for 2 to 3 minutes to heat through, spooning the stir-fry and its sauce over the top of the fillets. Carefully transfer to a platter and garnish with the red pepper and cilantro.

DEEP-FRIED POMFRET, KAMPOT STYLE
Trey Chap Kampot

SERVES 4

This recipe for deep-fried fish with a spicy sauce is a specialty of the coastal region, from the area around the town of Kampot. *Trey Chap* literally means "bird fish" in Khmer, but the more common name is pomfret. If you can't find this small tasty flatfish, substitute sole, perch or tilapia.

½ cup fresh lime juice
½ cup fish sauce
¼ cup sugar
1 garlic clove, smashed and coarsely chopped
3 bird's eye chilies, thinly sliced and seeded (or
     retain the seeds if you want the dish very hot)
4 whole pomfret (about 2 pounds), cleaned
Vegetable oil, for frying
Thinly sliced cucumbers, for garnish

Combine the lime juice, fish sauce and sugar in a small bowl and mix until the sugar dissolves completely. Stir in the garlic and chilies and set aside.

Rinse the fish inside and out, then pat dry with paper towels.

Heat about 4 inches oil in a wok or large deep skillet over medium-high heat. When the oil is hot, fry the fish in batches, turning once, until well browned and crisp, about 5 minutes per side. Remove with a slotted spoon and drain on paper towels, then cover to keep warm.

When all the fish is fried, transfer to a large platter. Spoon the sauce over the fish and garnish with sliced cucumbers.

ROYAL CATFISH ENROBED WITH COCONUT MILK AND LEMONGRASS
Trey Trung Kroeung

SERVES 4

PASTE

3 dried New Mexico chilies, soaked, seeded and
   deveined

1 tablespoon sliced lemongrass

3 garlic cloves, coarsely chopped

2 medium shallots, coarsely chopped

5 kaffir lime leaves, deveined

2 teaspoons peeled, coarsely chopped galangal

¼ teaspoon turmeric

1½ teaspoons shrimp paste

½ cup water

6 tablespoons vegetable oil

4 catfish fillets (about 2 pounds)

1½ cups unsweetened coconut milk

1 tablespoon fish sauce

2 teaspoons sugar

4 kaffir lime leaves, deveined and julienned

As the name indicates, this dish is considered very fancy, and in Cambodia when I was growing up, it was served only in aristocratic homes for festive occasions. But for all of its elegant appearance and rich sauce, Royal Catfish is actually quite simple to make when you have a blender. The spice paste can be prepared quickly, the fish is fried and all that remains is to cover the fish in its succulent "robe." Royalty has rarely been achieved so easily.

TO MAKE THE PASTE: Put all the paste ingredients in a blender and blend until smooth, 2 to 3 minutes. Set aside.

Heat ¼ cup of the oil in a large skillet over medium-high heat. Fry the fish until firm and golden brown, turning once, about 6 minutes per side. Set aside, covered, to keep warm.

In a second large skillet, heat the remaining 2 tablespoons oil. Add ½ cup of the coconut milk and cook over medium-high heat until the oil separates from the coconut milk. Add

the paste and cook for about 2 minutes, stirring constantly, until the aroma is released. Add the remaining 1 cup coconut milk, fish sauce and sugar and cook for 5 minutes more, stirring all the while.

Remove from the heat and add the fish, spoon the sauce over the fillets to cover fully and allow to sit for 1 to 2 minutes. Carefully transfer the fish and sauce to a platter. Sprinkle the kaffir lime leaves over the top of the fish. Serve with rice.

CURRIED CATFISH
Curry Trey Ruah

SERVES 4

This complex curried fish is Indian in its origin, but very Cambodian in its interpretation, using shrimp paste and lemongrass. For convenience, I usually buy the whole cinnamon, nutmeg, anise and cardamom for this recipe together in a single package at an Asian market. Frozen mudfish would be my first choice here, but both catfish and snapper make a fine showing, and shrimp is also delicious. (Use 1 to 1½ pounds of jumbo shrimp, shelled and deveined.)

PASTE

1 tablespoon vegetable oil

3 dried New Mexico chilies, soaked, seeded, deveined and chopped into 1-inch pieces

1 cinnamon stick, broken into pieces

½ Asian nutmeg

2 whole star anise

5 cardamom seeds

½ stalk lemongrass, thinly sliced

2 tablespoons coarsely chopped fresh cilantro

4 large garlic cloves, coarsely chopped

2 medium shallots, coarsely chopped

1 tablespoon peeled, coarsely chopped galangal

2 pieces rhizome, each about 2½ inches long

1 cup water

2 teaspoons shrimp paste

¼ teaspoon turmeric

3 tablespoons vegetable oil

1½ cups unsweetened coconut milk

¼ cup tamarind juice

2½ tablespoons sugar

2 tablespoons fish sauce

1 teaspoon salt

1½ pounds catfish or snapper fillets, cut into quarters, or 2½ pounds whole mudfish, cleaned and sliced crosswise into 1-inch-wide pieces

½ pound eggplant (preferably the long, slender purple variety), cut on the diagonal into 1-inch slices

¼ pound string beans, cut into 2-inch pieces

Thinly sliced bird's eye chilies

TO MAKE THE PASTE: Heat the oil in a large heavy skillet over medium-high heat and gently stir in the chilies, cinnamon, nutmeg, star anise, cardamom, lemongrass, cilantro, garlic, shallots, galangal and rhizome. Cook until they are browned and give off a roasted aroma, 6 to 7 minutes. Transfer the herbs and spices to a blender, add the water, shrimp paste and turmeric and blend until smooth, 2 to 3 minutes. Set aside.

Heat the oil in the same skillet over medium-high heat, add the coconut milk and cook until the oil begins to separate from the milk, 2 to 3 minutes. Add the spice paste, tamarind juice, sugar, fish sauce and salt and cook for about 4 minutes to blend the flavors. Gently stir in the fish, eggplant and string beans, turning to coat, and cook until the fish is tender, 5 to 7 minutes.

Serve with rice and sliced bird's eye chilies on the side.

CARAMELIZED WHITE FISH WITH FRIED GARLIC

Khar Trey Ruah Nung Saik Chrouk

SERVES 4

In this braise, slices of firm white fish are cooked in a rich caramelized sauce, infused with the taste of pork, fried garlic and pepper. It's a delicious dish that has an elegant look to it but is simple to prepare. Whatever kind of fish you use (and I have even had it made with mackerel, which was splendid), try to keep the pieces whole while cooking. I like to accompany the dish with rice and any of the pickles in this book.

2 pounds whole cleaned mudfish or 1½ pounds firm freshwater fish fillets, such as catfish or tilapia

¼ cup fish sauce

1 tablespoon mushroom soy sauce

2 tablespoons vegetable oil

5 garlic cloves, smashed and coarsely chopped

5 tablespoons sugar

½ pound pork tenderloin or fresh ham, cut into pieces 1½ inches long, 1½ inches wide and ¼ inch thick

2 cups water

2 teaspoons salt

2 teaspoons freshly ground pepper

1 scallion, cut into ¼-inch pieces

Slice the fish crosswise into 1½-inch-wide pieces. Marinate the fish in the fish sauce and soy sauce for 15 to 20 minutes.

Meanwhile, heat the oil in a large heavy skillet over medium-high heat and sauté the garlic until just starting to brown, 5 to 10 seconds. Reduce the heat to medium, add the sugar and stir constantly as it liquifies, browns and froths, 3 to 4 minutes. When the caramel is dark brown but not burned, add the pork and cook for 5 minutes, stirring occasionally.

Carefully add the fish and its marinade, being careful not

to break up the fish, and cook for 2 minutes. Add the water, salt and pepper, reduce the heat to medium-low and cook for 25 minutes, or until the pork is tender. If the sauce is too thick, add a few tablespoons of water. Carefully transfer to a serving platter, sprinkle with scallion and serve immediately.

STEAMED FISH WITH LILIES
Trey Chamhoy

SERVES 4

This is one of the subtler dishes in the Cambodian repertoire, in which all of the ingredients, from the delicate fish to the tender mushrooms, are understated and mild. As a consequence, the dish is often served as the focal point for other, spicier foods, and at the very least it should be served with chilies. In Cambodia, we make this recipe with *trey domrei,* which means elephant fish — a firm white fish that is perfect for steaming — but catfish and the other firm white fish like tilapia, sole or snapper, which are readily available in the United States, work just as well.

1 small package (1¾ ounces) bean thread noodles
¼ ounce small black fungus
15 dried lilies (about ½ ounce)
2 pounds whole tilapia, cleaned, or
    1½ pounds catfish fillets
½ cup peeled, julienned ginger (about 2 ounces)
3 tablespoons salted soybeans, mashed slightly
2 tablespoons mushroom soy sauce
2 tablespoons sugar
1 teaspoon salt
2 scallions, sliced diagonally into 2-inch pieces
¼ teaspoon freshly ground pepper
Julienned red bell pepper

———

Soak the bean thread noodles, black fungus and dried lilies separately in lukewarm water to cover for about 15 minutes; drain.

Fill the bottom of a steamer with water and bring to a boil. Put the fish on a large bowl or plate with high sides that will fit into the steamer. If using fillets, cut into quarters and arrange so they don't overlap.

Cut the bean thread noodles into 2-inch lengths. Scrape off any dirt from the black fungus and cut out the hard stem. Tie the lily flowers into knots.

Mix the noodles, fungus and lily flowers together in a bowl, then add the ginger, soybeans, soy sauce, sugar and salt. Spoon over the fish, and sprinkle with scallions and black pepper. Top with the red pepper. Place in the steamer, cover and steam for 30 to 45 minutes, or until the fish is firm. Serve immediately.

SHRIMP WITH DAIKON
Khar B'kong Chai Peoah

SERVES 4

1 tablespoon mushroom soy sauce

1½ teaspoons fish sauce

½ teaspoon freshly ground pepper

8 jumbo shrimp, peeled and deveined

1 cup preserved daikon, rinsed

3 tablespoons vegetable oil

3 garlic cloves, smashed and coarsely chopped

3 tablespoons sugar

2½ cups chicken broth

In a medium bowl, mix together the soy sauce, fish sauce and pepper. Add the shrimp and set aside to marinate for 10 minutes. Meanwhile, thinly slice the daikon on the diagonal. Soak the daikon in several cups of water to remove saltiness, if necessary; drain.

Heat the oil in a large heavy skillet over medium-high heat and sauté the garlic until golden, 5 to 10 seconds. Reduce the heat to medium, add the sugar and cook, stirring constantly, as it liquifies, browns and froths, 3 to 4 minutes.

Add the shrimp and stir to coat with the caramel. Add the chicken broth and bring to a boil. Add the daikon slices, return to a boil, stirring occasionally, and continue cooking until the shrimp is opaque, 5 to 6 minutes. Remove from the heat and serve immediately.

Preserved daikon is the signature flavor of this dish, a complement to the sweet flavor and firm texture of the shrimp, and I am always inclined to add extra because I like it so much. We used to make our own — a long process of repeated saltings and rinsings that ended with packing the daikon slices in jars with palm sugar. But the store-bought version is fine; just be sure to taste it first, and if it's too salty, soak the slices in water. Because rice also cuts saltiness, it is considered the perfect accompaniment for this dish.

SAUTÉED MUSSELS WITH BASIL
Leah Cha

SERVES 4

This charming dish makes a lovely addition to any meal. In Cambodia, it would be made with wonderful sweet-tasting freshwater clams that come from the Tonle Sap Lake, but I am very satisfied with the substitution of mussels.

1 tablespoon vegetable oil

3 garlic cloves, coarsely chopped

3 dozen mussels (preferably cultivated), scrubbed well and beards removed

2 teaspoons sugar

1 teaspoon salt

2 cups loosely packed fresh basil leaves

1½ teaspoons seeded chopped bird's eye chilies

¾ cup julienned red bell pepper

2 scallions, cut into 1-inch pieces

In a large wok, heat the oil over medium-high heat and sauté the garlic until golden, 5 to 10 seconds. Add the mussels, sprinkle the sugar and salt over them and stir well. Cover and cook for about 5 minutes, shaking the pan constantly until all of the shells have opened. Stir in the basil, chilies, red pepper and scallions until well combined. Discard any unopened mussels and serve immediately.

STIR-FRIED SHRIMP WITH SNOW PEAS
Cha How Lang Tao Nung B'kong

SERVES 4

Like all stir-fries, this dish is a simple meal at heart but exceptionally tasty. The pink of the shrimp looks very pretty with the green of the peas, and you will get the same effect if you substitute lobster for the shrimp.

¾ pound medium shrimp, shelled and deveined
3 tablespoons vegetable oil
4 garlic cloves, smashed
1 pound snow peas, stems and strings removed
3 tablespoons fish sauce
1½ tablespoons sugar
¼ teaspoon freshly ground pepper

Butterfly the shrimp by cutting them down the back lengthwise but not all the way through, so they will flare open when cooked.

Heat the oil in a large skillet or wok over medium-high heat and sauté the garlic until golden, 5 to 10 seconds. Stirring well after each addition, add the shrimp, peas, fish sauce and sugar and cook until the snow peas have lost their crunch but are not yet mushy, 5 to 6 minutes. Add the pepper and serve immediately.

FOWL

CAMBODIANS USE LOTS OF FOWL IN THEIR cooking, particularly in the simpler dishes: in stir-fries, in basic soups and on the grill. You can't find a marketplace in Cambodia where chicken isn't being grilled as a matter of course. The reason for the popularity of this food is simple: nothing is more heavenly than the indigenous Grilled Chicken with Lemongrass, especially when enjoyed with light, lemony pickled vegetables and cold fruit juice. The subtler Classic Cambodian Chicken and Rice and French-Style Chicken with Rice are both culinary manifestations of colonial influence.

For all these dishes, what we value most is a flavorful bird, which we tend to take for granted, because all our chickens are free-range and allowed to mature. (Here, I seek out certified free-range or kosher chickens to get the same results.) We prize not only the rich-tasting meat, but also the bones. They are essential for making broths — very important in a cuisine that includes as much soup as ours. Because of their full flavor, we prefer the moist dark meat and legs. For the same reason, we generally cook our birds with the bones in, using a cleaver to cut the desired bite-sized pieces.

From the simplest grilled chicken to a deliciously elaborate curry, the Cambodian approach to fowl, whether stir-fried, steamed, roasted or boiled, is an enriching addition to any repertoire.

CAMBODIAN GRILLED CHICKEN
Mouan Ang

SERVES 4

¼ cup mushroom soy sauce

2 tablespoons sugar

4 garlic cloves, smashed and coarsely chopped

1 tablespoon vegetable oil

1 teaspoon freshly ground pepper

½ teaspoon salt

8 chicken legs

In a large bowl, combine the soy sauce, sugar, garlic, oil, pepper and salt. Apply this moist rub to the chicken legs with your fingers until the legs are well coated, then set aside for 30 minutes.

Preheat the grill or broiler, positioning a rack about 6 inches from the heat. Grill or broil the chicken for 25 to 30 minutes, turning occasionally, until golden brown and cooked through. Serve hot.

My family used to go on holiday to a small town called Kep, on the coast of the Gulf of Siam. Lots of wonderful restaurants lined the beach, and grilled chicken was one of the specialties. This recipe calls for chicken legs, but breasts work just as well, as would two small game hens, about one pound each, split down the middle and scored on the inside to allow the marinade to penetrate. *Mouan Ang* tastes best when grilled outside.

GRILLED CORNISH HENS WITH LEMONGRASS
Mouan Ang Kroeung

SERVES 4

> Permeated with the rich flavor of lemongrass, these broiled Cornish hens go well with rice and pickles — particularly Mixed Vegetable Pickles (page 256) — and clear soup. The flavor of the paste will infuse the hens even when they are marinated for only a short time, but they will have more flavor if you can let them sit overnight.

PASTE

3 tablespoons sliced lemongrass

3 garlic cloves, coarsely chopped

1 small shallot, coarsely chopped

2 teaspoons chopped fresh cilantro stems

¼ teaspoon turmeric

1 tablespoon peeled, coarsely chopped galangal

⅓ cup water

3 tablespoons sugar

2½ teaspoons salt

2 Cornish hens (1¼–1½ pounds each), cut in half and wing tips tucked under

TO MAKE THE PASTE: Blend all the ingredients in a blender until smooth, 2 to 3 minutes.

Pour the paste into a large bowl and stir in the sugar and salt. Add the Cornish hens, turning to coat, and let sit for at least 15 minutes and as long as overnight; refrigerate if marinating for more than 30 minutes.

Preheat the grill or broiler, positioning a rack about 4 inches from the heat. Grill or broil until well browned all over and cooked through, 10 to 12 minutes per side. Serve hot.

GINGER CHICKEN
Mouan Cha K'nyei

SERVES 4

3 tablespoons vegetable oil

2 garlic cloves, smashed

1¼ cups peeled, finely julienned ginger
    (about 5 ounces)

1 pound boneless skinless chicken breasts, cut on the
    diagonal into ¼-inch-thick slices

1½ tablespoons fish sauce

1½ tablespoons mushroom soy sauce

4 teaspoons sugar

¼ teaspoon salt

1 medium onion (about 5 ounces), sliced into
    ¼-inch-thick wedges

2 scallions, cut into 1½-inch pieces

¼ red bell pepper, julienned

I like the peppery quality of ginger, and it's particularly nice in this stir-fry, balanced by the sweetness of fried garlic and onion. The sauce, which gets its rich brown color from the mushroom soy sauce, tastes great over rice.

Heat the oil in a large skillet or wok over medium-high heat. Add the garlic and ginger and cook until brown and crisp, 4 to 5 minutes.

Stirring well after each addition, add the chicken, fish sauce, soy sauce, sugar and salt. When these ingredients are thoroughly blended, add the onion, scallions and red pepper and cook, stirring well, for 1 to 2 minutes more, until the chicken is cooked and the vegetables are heated through. Serve with rice.

CLASSIC CAMBODIAN CHICKEN AND RICE

Bai Mouan

SERVES 4 TO 6

- 4 quarts water
- 2 teaspoons salt
- 1 chicken (3½ pounds), preferably free-range or kosher
- 2 tablespoons vegetable oil
- 6 garlic cloves, smashed and finely chopped
- 3 cups jasmine rice, rinsed and drained

DIPPING SAUCE

- Juice and pulp of 1½ limes
- 6 garlic cloves, ground to a paste with a mortar and pestle or mini-chop
- 1½ teaspoons chopped red bell pepper
- 1 or more bird's eye chilies to taste, finely chopped (optional)
- ¼ cup fish sauce
- 1 tablespoon sugar

- 1 small onion, very thinly sliced
- 2 tablespoons preserved cabbage (optional)
- 1 English cucumber, thinly sliced
- 1 small head green leaf lettuce, separated, washed, dried and torn into small pieces
- 1 scallion, sliced ¼ inch thick

This dish has everything: tender chicken, fluffy rice, rich broth, a light salad, interesting condiments and a lively garlic and lime juice sauce, all prepared in such a way that every serving can be made completely to taste — a personal culinary masterpiece. Traditionally, the broth is drunk separately or spooned over the chicken and rice in order to cleanse and moisten the palate, but it can just as easily become a soup base to which the other ingredients are added. Using a free-range or kosher chicken in this recipe guarantees that both bird and broth will be richly flavored; otherwise, you should add extra chicken bones, like backs and necks, to the broth. I like to spice up this dish with some bird's eye chilies, but you may choose to omit them.

In a large stockpot over high heat, bring the water with the salt to a boil. Add the chicken, return the water to a boil and skim off any foam. Reduce the heat to low and simmer until the chicken is just tender, 30 to 35 minutes. Set the chicken aside to cool and keep the broth warm over low heat.

In a large deep skillet or wok, heat the oil and sauté the

garlic over medium-high heat until brown but not burned, 5 to 10 seconds. Add the rice and sauté until the grains become opaque, 4 to 5 minutes. Add 5 cups of the chicken broth to the skillet or wok (you may wish to transfer the rice and garlic and broth to a rice cooker) and cook until tender.

TO MAKE THE DIPPING SAUCE: Combine all the ingredients in a small serving bowl.

In another serving bowl, mix the onion and preserved cabbage (if using) and cover with the remaining warm broth. Put the rice in a third serving bowl. Cut the chicken into bite-sized pieces and arrange them on a platter with the cucumber, lettuce, and scallions. To make an individual serving, put pieces of chicken, rice, cucumbers and lettuce in your own bowl and add dipping sauce to taste. Sprinkle with some scallions. Ladle the broth mixed with onions and preserved cabbage over all.

FRENCH-STYLE CHICKEN WITH RICE
Poulet au Riz

SERVES 4 TO 6

2½ teaspoons salt

½ teaspoon freshly ground pepper

1 chicken (2½ pounds), preferably free-range or
  kosher

6 tablespoons vegetable oil

6 garlic cloves, smashed

1 cup water

1 small onion, cut into ¼-inch-thick wedges

2 tablespoons tomato paste

4 cups cooked jasmine rice (page 295)

Thinly sliced tomatoes, for garnish

This is a classic recipe for chicken pan-roasted in the original French style — an old-fashioned method of frying that you can still find some people in France using today. Cambodians added flavored rice to the dish and made it their own, and time was when you could go to any restaurant in the resort towns along the Gulf of Siam and get a wonderful *Poulet au Riz*. This dish is terrific with a green salad topped with lots of thinly sliced onions and a simple dressing. (If you don't have cooked rice on hand, you may want to make this your first step.)

Rub 1 teaspoon of the salt and the pepper all over the chicken, inside and out. Tie the legs together and tuck the wings under, to ensure even cooking. Set aside.

Heat 3 tablespoons of the oil in a large skillet or wok over medium-high heat, add 2 of the garlic cloves and cook until well browned, 5 to 10 seconds. Remove the garlic and reserve.

Cook the chicken in the garlic-flavored oil, turning every couple of minutes, until the chicken is browned all over, 10 to 15 minutes. Transfer the chicken to a large wide pot with a cover. Drain the oil from the skillet and deglaze the pan with the water mixed with ½ teaspoon of the salt. Pour the liquid over the chicken, distribute the onion around it and sprinkle the bird with the cooked garlic. Cover the chicken and simmer for 35 to 40 minutes.

Meanwhile, wipe out the skillet or wok and heat the remaining 3 tablespoons oil in it over medium-high heat. Sauté the remaining 4 garlic cloves until golden brown, 5 to 10 seconds. Add the tomato paste, cooked rice and the remaining 1 teaspoon salt and cook, stirring, until the rice is heated through, 3 to 4 minutes.

To serve, place the chicken on a platter with the rice mounded next to it. Garnish with slices of tomatoes.

STEAMED CHICKEN
Mouan Chamhoy

SERVES 4

1½–2 pounds chicken pieces (preferably 2 whole
    legs and 1 whole breast), cut into 1½-inch
    lengths

1 tablespoon fish sauce

1½ teaspoons sugar

¼ teaspoon salt

¼ cup pickled scallions or pickled garlic

2 tablespoons vegetable oil

1 large shallot, thinly sliced

½ pound pickled mustard greens (store-bought or
    homemade; see page 259)

½ pound plum tomatoes (about 3 medium), halved,
    seeds squeezed out and sliced ½ inch thick

¼ cup peeled ginger, julienned (about 1 ounce)

Every bite of this chicken casserole offers a new treat — the sweetness of the pickled garlic or scallions here, the tangy bite of the mustard greens there. And they all blend together to make a wonderful juicy broth that tastes great with the chicken and spooned over rice. With its layers of ingredients and colors, Steamed Chicken is a fitting dish to serve to guests — and particularly special if you make the pickled mustard greens yourself.

Fill the bottom of a large steamer with water and bring to a boil. While the water is heating, toss the chicken pieces with the fish sauce, sugar and salt and set aside to marinate. Thinly slice the pickled scallions; or if using pickled garlic, peel the skins off the cloves.

Heat the oil in a small skillet over medium-high heat and sauté the shallot slices until brown but not burned, 2 to 3 minutes. Set aside.

Put the chicken in a casserole dish that will fit into the steamer. Cover with the mustard greens, then the tomatoes, then the pickled scallions or garlic and the ginger and top with the reserved fried shallot.

Put the casserole dish into the steamer, cover and steam for 1 hour, or until the chicken is tender. Serve immediately.

FIVE-SPICE CHICKEN WITH DATES
Mouan Tum

SERVES 4

STUFFING

⅓ cup dried lotus seeds, soaked in warm water for
    at least 1 hour, or overnight, and drained

½ ounce dried shiitake mushrooms, soaked in 1½
    cups warm water for 30 minutes, or until
    spongy, and drained; 1 cup soaking water
    reserved

4–5 ounces bean thread noodles, soaked in warm
    water for 10–15 minutes and drained

5 tablespoons vegetable oil

12 garlic cloves, 2 smashed, 10 left whole

¼ pound ground pork (optional)

¼ cup sugar

3 tablespoons mushroom soy sauce

2 tablespoons fish sauce

2 teaspoons salt

3 large shallots, sliced in half

15 Chinese red dates (about 1 ounce)

1½ teaspoons five-spice powder

35–40 medium dried shrimp (about ½ ounce),
    optional

2 Cornish hens (3–3½ pounds), split in half

½ teaspoon salt

½ teaspoon freshly ground pepper

3 tablespoons vegetable oil

2 cups chicken broth or water

2 scallions, cut into 1-inch pieces, for garnish

Cilantro sprigs, for garnish

This dish delicately balances many wonderful flavors around a chicken-with-stuffing theme. The stuffing includes ingredients with some of the most interesting textures and flavors of Southeast Asia, such as lotus seeds, shiitake mushrooms, bean thread noodles, Chinese red dates and dried shrimp. The traditional way to prepare the dish is to steam whole chickens stuffed with the noodle mixture, but my family prefers this version of layering split Cornish hens with the other ingredients. There is some advanced preparation required, involving mostly soaking, and a number of ingredients to be gathered together, but otherwise the recipe is a straightforward preparation. See the photograph on page 190.

To make the stuffing: In a small saucepan, boil the soaked lotus seeds in water to cover until soft but not mushy, about 30 minutes; drain and set aside.

Slice the soaked mushrooms into 1-inch pieces and set aside, along with the 1 cup reserved soaking liquid. Cut the bean thread noodles into 2-inch pieces and set aside.

In a large skillet, heat the oil over high heat and fry the smashed garlic cloves until golden brown, 5 to 10 seconds. Add the pork (if using), breaking it apart as it cooks, 1 to 2 minutes. Stir in the sugar, soy sauce, fish sauce, salt, shallots, dates, five-spice powder, dried shrimp (if using) and the remaining 10 whole garlic cloves. Stir in the cooked lotus seeds, the mushrooms and noodles and cook for about 5 minutes, until the flavors have melded. Transfer the stuffing to a bowl and deglaze the skillet with the reserved mushroom liquid; set the liquid aside.

Sprinkle the hen halves with the salt and the pepper. In a large skillet, heat the oil over high heat, add the hens, without crowding (you may need to fry them in two batches), and cook until golden brown on both sides, about 6 minutes altogether. Arrange 2 of the hen halves in the bottom of a large pot, cover with half the stuffing and repeat with a second layer of chicken and stuffing.

Deglaze the skillet with 1 cup of the broth or water; add to this the reserved cup of mushroom deglazing liquid, along with the remaining cup of broth or water. Pour all 3 cups of liquid over the chicken and stuffing, swirling the pot to distribute the flavors. Bring the liquid to a boil, reduce the heat and simmer, partially covered, until the Cornish hens are tender, 40 to 45 minutes.

Transfer to a serving dish and garnish with the scallions and cilantro.

FIVE-SPICE CHICKEN
WITH DATES

CHICKEN STIR-FRY WITH GINGER, ONIONS AND SCALLIONS
Mouan K'chop

SERVES 4

½ cup vegetable oil

1½–2 pounds boneless chicken thighs, cut into
    2-inch pieces and sliced ½ inch thick

½ cup peeled, julienned ginger (about 2 ounces)

4 large garlic cloves, smashed and coarsely chopped

1 tablespoon hoisin sauce

2 teaspoons mushroom soy sauce

1 teaspoon fish sauce

1 medium onion, cut into quarters and thinly sliced
    (about 1 cup)

2 scallions, cut into 1½-inch pieces

2 tablespoons thinly sliced pickled scallions

2 tablespoons water

Cilantro sprigs, for garnish

Chicken provides a perfect backdrop for the peppery bite of the ginger and the sweetness of the garlic, onions and scallions. The Chinese make this dish by wrapping the ingredients in paper and frying, but it is easier prepared in this fashion.

Heat the oil in a large skillet over medium-high heat. Add the chicken, in batches, and fry until opaque and lightly browned all over, 4 to 5 minutes, transferring the chicken to a plate as it's done. Pour off all but 2 tablespoons of the oil and return the skillet to the heat.

Add the ginger and garlic and cook, stirring, until brown, 2 to 3 minutes. Return the chicken to the skillet and stir in the hoisin sauce, soy sauce and fish sauce. Add the onion, scallions and pickled scallions, tossing well. Stir in the water and cook until the sauce is warmed though and the chicken is tender, 1 to 2 minutes. Garnish with cilantro and serve.

CHICKEN CURRY
Curry Mouan

Chicken Curry is not an everyday event: it is too rich and it requires too many ingredients to be a casual meal. But when we have something to celebrate, we always think of this curry, with its magnificent array of flavors. The look of a curry is important to Cambodians: we like to see lots of small dark spots of oil — dark red from the chili peppers — pooled on the surface of the sauce. Potatoes, which are especially delicious because they are fried before being added, balance out the richness, framing the various tastes. For this same reason, rice or good bread makes an excellent accompaniment.

SERVES 8

PASTE

¼ cup vegetable oil

¼ cup sliced lemongrass

3 dried New Mexico chilies, soaked, seeded and deveined

5 garlic cloves, coarsely chopped

1 large shallot, coarsely chopped

2 slices peeled galangal, about 1½ inches across and ⅛ inch thick

1½ cinnamon sticks, cracked

4 whole star anise

9 cardamom seeds

1 small Asian nutmeg

16 peppercorns

½ teaspoon coriander seeds

½ teaspoon fennel seeds

1 cup water

¼ cup coarsely chopped fresh cilantro stems

¼ teaspoon turmeric

2½ teaspoons shrimp paste

½ cup plus 1–2 tablespoons vegetable oil

3½ cups unsweetened coconut milk

1½–2 pounds chicken pieces (2 or 3 whole legs, cut into 1½-inch pieces, and 2 wings, severed at the joints with a cleaver)

1 medium onion, thinly sliced

2 tablespoons fish sauce

4 teaspoons sugar

1 teaspoon salt

1 pound Idaho potatoes, peeled, halved and cut into 1-inch-thick slices

To make the paste: Heat the oil in a large skillet over medium-high heat. Add all of the remaining paste ingredients and fry for about 5 minutes, until the flavors have been released.

With a slotted spoon, transfer the ingredients to a blender. Add the water, cilantro, turmeric and shrimp paste to the blender and blend until smooth, 2 to 3 minutes. Set aside.

In a large heavy pot, heat 1 tablespoon of the oil over medium-high heat. Add 1 cup of the coconut milk and cook until the oil begins to separate from the milk, 2 to 3 minutes. Add 1½ cups of the curry paste (freeze any extra for future use) and cook, stirring, for another 2 minutes while the spice flavors develop. If the surface of the sauce is not covered with dark spots, add another tablespoon of oil.

Add the chicken to the sauce, stirring well to coat, then add the onion, fish sauce, sugar and salt and cook for 5 minutes. Add the remaining 2½ cups coconut milk and cook at a high simmer, partially covered, until the chicken is tender, 20 to 25 minutes.

While the curry is cooking, heat the remaining ½ cup oil in a large skillet over medium-high heat. Add the potatoes and fry, turning, until golden brown, about 10 minutes.

Add the potatoes to the pot with the chicken and finish cooking until the chicken is done and the potatoes are tender. Transfer to a serving dish and serve with rice.

CAMBODIAN RATATOUILLE
Somlah Kako

SERVES 4

PASTE

2 stalks lemongrass, thinly sliced

8 kaffir lime leaves, deveined

5 garlic cloves, coarsely chopped

1 tablespoon peeled, coarsely chopped galangal

½ teaspoon turmeric

1½ cups water

½ pound green papaya, peeled and seeded
   (or unpeeled zucchini), cut into 2-inch chunks

½ pound buttercup squash or another similar
   winter squash, peeled, seeded and cut into
   2-inch chunks

½ pound eggplant, peeled and cut into
   2-inch chunks

½ pound string beans, cut into 2-inch lengths

1 large Cornish hen (about 2 pounds), cut into
   bite-sized pieces with a cleaver

1–2 tablespoons *prahok*, to taste

¼ cup roasted rice powder (optional)

2½ tablespoons fish sauce

1 teaspoon salt

½ teaspoon sugar

2 cups water

¼ pound Chinese spinach leaves, torn into bite-
   sized pieces (regular spinach or radish greens can
   be substituted)

Thinly sliced bird's eye chilies

This hearty stew of vegetables and Cornish hen gets its distinctively Khmer taste from roasted rice, lemongrass and *prahok*. The traditional way to make Cambodian Ratatouille is with catfish, but I prefer Cornish hens, and I have found that free-range chicken and quail — or even the vegetables alone — are also very good. When I was growing up, I used to pile on the *prahok* and chilies for really strong flavor, but for those with Western palates, I recommend greater restraint, at least to start. However strong you like it, I think rice is essential with this dish.

TO MAKE THE PASTE: Combine all the ingredients in a blender and blend until smooth, 2 to 3 minutes.

Combine the papaya (or zucchini), squash, eggplant and

beans in a large stockpot over medium-high heat. Add the Cornish hen, spice paste and the *prahok* and stir constantly for about 5 minutes, until the vegetables and bird are well coated.

Add the roasted rice powder (if using), fish sauce, salt, sugar and water, stirring well. Cook at a simmer until the vegetables are soft and the chicken is tender, 10 to 12 minutes, stirring occasionally. Stir in the Chinese spinach and serve with lots of chilies.

BRAISED DUCK
Hong Tiah

SERVES 8

1 duck (5–6 pounds), cut into serving-sized pieces
   with a cleaver, visible fat removed
2 teaspoons salt
1½ teaspoons freshly ground pepper
⅓ cup vegetable oil
3 large shallots, thinly sliced
20 garlic cloves, 15 thinly sliced, 5 left whole
2 tablespoons salted soybeans
5 cups water
3 tablespoons fish sauce
1 tablespoon mushroom soy sauce
1 teaspoon five-spice powder
5 tablespoons sugar
20 small dried shiitake mushrooms (about 1 ounce),
   soaked in warm water for 10 minutes, drained
   and stems removed
Cilantro sprigs for garnish

In this braised duck dish, the broth blends a host of different tastes into such a unified masterpiece that it shares center stage with the duck itself. You'll really want to serve this dish with rice, and Tomato Salad (page 229) goes particularly well with it also. Otherwise, there's so much flavor here that you don't need anything more than sliced cucumbers to round out a perfect meal.

Rub the duck with the salt and pepper and set aside.

Heat the oil in a large skillet or wok over medium-high heat and fry the shallots until softened and brown, about 5 minutes. Remove with a slotted spoon and set aside. In the same oil, fry the 15 sliced garlic cloves until brown, about 2 minutes; remove and reserve the garlic and set the pan aside, leaving the oil in the pan.

In a small dry skillet, pan-roast the remaining 5 whole garlic cloves over medium heat until lightly browned all over, 5 to 10 minutes. Put the fried shallots and all the garlic in a blender or food processor with the salted soybeans and 1 cup of the water and blend until smooth, 2 to 3 minutes.

Reheat the oil over medium-high heat and sear the duck, a few pieces at a time, until lightly browned all over. Transfer the duck and its juices to a stockpot and add the fish sauce, soy sauce, five-spice powder, sugar and the shallot-garlic paste. Deglaze the pan the duck was cooked in with the remaining 4 cups water and add to the stockpot.

Bring to a boil, skim any foam, reduce the heat to low and simmer, partially covered, until the duck is tender, about 1 hour. Add the shiitake mushrooms during the last 20 minutes. When the braise is done, skim off and discard any fat and transfer to a serving bowl. Serve garnished with cilantro.

RICE AND NOODLES

RICE AND NOODLES FORM THE BASIS OF THE carbohydrate-rich Asian diet and are central to the culture. The Khmer phrase *n'yam bai,* "to eat," literally translated, means "to eat rice," and a Cambodian host always invites a guest to eat rice no matter what the meal. (The same is true of eating and language customs throughout Southeast Asia.) In one form or another, rice defines a Cambodian meal, and the meal is considered incomplete if it doesn't include either rice or rice noodles.

This staple is nearly sacred. Children are taught not to step on it, and Khmers consider it a sacrilege to throw it away. It is not surprising, then, to find a number of dishes that make use of leftover rice. Crispy Rice is one popular example of this practice. These deliciously crackling rice cakes are made from the grains left sticking to the bottom of the cooking pot. They are enjoyed plain but also with other, more elegant fare like Red Pork with Coconut Milk (page 52).

The centrality of rice is nearly matched by that of rice noodles, despite the fact that they are much newer to our table. Everywhere you look — on street corners in Phnom Penh, at stalls in the Siem Reap market, along the road to Kampot — at any time of day, you're likely to see people eating or selling the flat noodles. They may have come with the Chinese who settled in Cambodia (which is why we use Chinese chopsticks to eat them), but we have taken them to heart.

The rice and noodle recipes that follow come largely from the tradition of street foods and are dishes that can be prepared as part of a larger meal or eaten as meals in themselves. They make up some of the quickest, lightest and cleverest dishes in the Cambodian repertoire.

CRISPY RICE
Bai K'dong

SERVES 8

4 cups cooked jasmine rice (page 295)
4–5 cups vegetable oil

———

Loosely spread the rice out in the bottom of a nonstick skillet (or a pan sprayed with vegetable oil) to a depth of ¼ inch; you can either use one pan and cook the rice in batches or use more than one pan and cook it all at once. Add water just to cover and begin cooking over low heat. With a spoon dipped into cold water (this will keep the rice from sticking to the spoon), press down gently on the rice as it cooks to help make it adhere to itself, being careful not to break the grains.

As the water evaporates, the rice will become shinier and more opaque and will start sticking together. If the rice remains separate in spots, spoon on a little extra water and press down some more. The rice is nearly done when it doesn't stick to a dry spoon; it is completely done when it lifts easily off the bottom of the pan as a single cake. Depending on the size of the pan, the cooking process should take about 15 to 20 minutes.

TO DRY THE RICE: Preheat the oven to 200°F. Put the rice cakes on cookie sheets and bake for 45 to 60 minutes, until fully dry. (In a warm, dry climate, it is possible to set the cakes aside to dry in a warm place where the air circulates, but that can take as long as 2 days.) Store the dried rice in an airtight container, to be fried as needed (it will keep for several months).

TO MAKE THE RICE "CRISPY": Add enough oil to a large pot, skillet or wok to deep-fry; the oil should be at least 2 to 3 inches deep. Heat the oil to between 375° and

Crispy Rice, the cracker-crisp appetizer of puffed rice that we serve at The Elephant Walk, is so light and delicious that you will always wish you had made more. It tastes terrific with spreads like Ginger Pork with Peanuts (page 43) or Red Pork with Coconut Milk (page 52), but it's almost as good plain. In Cambodia, *Bai K'dong*, literally "rice rind," is made from the rice left at the bottom of the cooking pot, which is dried in the hot sun and then either eaten with a small stir-fry or deep-fried into Crispy Rice. I've streamlined the technique for Western cooks. If you don't have time for this recipe, you can buy squares of "Instant Sizzling Rice" in Asian markets. Made from sticky rice, these rice cakes will have a slightly sweeter flavor but are still quite tasty. See the photograph on page 145.

400°F, testing for the correct temperature by putting in a small piece of rice cake: if it puffs up immediately and rises to the surface, the oil is just right.

Break the cakes into 2-to-3-inch pieces and drop several at a time into the hot oil, pressing down on each piece and swishing through the oil to cook all the grains — the pieces will puff noticeably. Turn, let cook a few seconds longer, until very light brown, and remove to a paper towel to drain. Puffing the rice takes only about 20 seconds for small pieces and 40 for large ones, so be careful not to overcook. Serve warm.

RICE CAKE TREAT
Bai K'dong K'tum

SERVES I

1 2-to-3-inch rice cake (page 203), cooked in the pan
    and still hot but not dried or deep-fried

2 tablespoons vegetable oil

1 scallion, thinly sliced

1 tablespoon water

1 tablespoon sugar

1 teaspoon fish sauce

½ teaspoon salt

> Both salty and sweet, this snack is made with the cooked rice "rinds" used to make Crispy Rice and a scallion-flavored sauce that takes only a minute to put together.

Transfer the warm rice cake to a serving dish. While it is cooling slightly, heat the oil in a small skillet over high heat. Add the remaining ingredients and stir-fry until the scallion begins to wilt, about 30 seconds. Spread over the rice cake and serve.

FRIED RICE WITH PORK SAUSAGE
Bai Laen Saik Krok

SERVES 4 GENEROUSLY

I love to make this fried rice because it looks so festive and people enjoy it so much. What really makes the difference here is the Chinese sausage, which is wonderfully salty but also sweet — it's almost addictive. This dish goes perfectly with a simply dressed salad and good French bread, and I always serve it with one of the vegetable pickles.

3 tablespoons vegetable oil
5 garlic cloves, smashed and coarsely chopped
¼ pound Chinese sausage, sliced ⅛ inch thick
3 large eggs, lightly whisked
1½ teaspoons salt
6 cups cooked jasmine rice (page 295)
2 scallions, thinly sliced

Heat the oil in a large skillet or wok over medium-high heat. Stir in the garlic and sausage, then add the eggs, stirring as they set up, and sprinkle with the salt. Fold in the rice, breaking apart any clumps to distribute it evenly. Stir in the scallions and cook until the rice is heated through, 3 to 4 minutes. Serve warm.

FRIED RICE WITH CRABMEAT
Bai Laen K'dom

Fresh crabmeat adds a wonderful sweetness to fried rice, but even canned crabmeat yields a delicious result. The flavor of the crab and garlic is mild and subtle overall, and the look of the dish is sophisticated. It tastes particularly good with Red Pepper Relish (page 255) or Pickled Bean Sprouts (page 253), and it's also terrific for breakfast.

SERVES 4 GENEROUSLY

3 tablespoons vegetable oil

5 garlic cloves, smashed and coarsely chopped

3 large eggs, lightly whisked

¾ pound fresh or canned crabmeat

2 teaspoons fish sauce

½ teaspoon salt

6 cups cooked jasmine rice (page 295)

2 scallions, thinly sliced

Heat the oil in a large skillet or wok over medium-high heat. Add the garlic and eggs, stirring as the eggs set up. Add the crabmeat, fish sauce and salt and mix well. Fold in the rice, breaking apart any clumps, then stir in the scallions and cook until the rice is heated through, 3 to 4 minutes. Serve warm.

SHRIMP FRIED RICE
Bai Laen B'kong

SERVES 4 GENEROUSLY

3 tablespoons vegetable oil

6 garlic cloves, crushed and coarsely chopped

¾ pound peeled black tiger shrimp, split lengthwise
   in half and then into quarters

2 scallions, thinly sliced

2 teaspoons fish sauce

1 teaspoon salt

6 cups cooked jasmine rice (page 295)

Heat the oil in a large skillet or wok over medium-high heat. Add the garlic and shrimp, stirring well. Add the scallions, fish sauce and salt and mix well. Fold in the rice, breaking apart any clumps, and cook until the shrimp is cooked and the rice is heated through, 3 to 4 minutes. Serve warm.

The quality of the shellfish is critical here, and the fresher it is, the sweeter it will taste. I usually make this dish with black tiger shrimp, which are firmer than regular shrimp and almost crunchy. For a nice garnish, cook a thin omelet of one or two eggs, slice it into narrow strips and sprinkle the yellow ribbons on top of the rice. Shiitake mushrooms are another special addition.

FRIED RICE WITH GARLIC
Bai Laen K'tem Sah

SERVES 4 TO 6

A cross between scrambled eggs with rice and a garlic omelet, this dish is an ingenious way to use leftover egg whites and cold rice. It's a particularly useful recipe for people watching their cholesterol. But more important than all of these practical matters, it tastes great.

3 tablespoons vegetable oil
¼ pound garlic cloves (30–40 cloves), smashed
5–6 egg whites (or whole eggs), lightly whisked
1½ teaspoons salt
6 cups cooked jasmine rice (page 295)

Heat the oil in a large skillet or wok over medium heat and sauté the garlic, stirring, until brown, 2 to 3 minutes. Reduce heat to low, add the egg whites and salt and cook, stirring, for about 45 seconds, until the eggs are soft but no longer wet. Stir in the rice, breaking apart any clumps, and cook until the rice is heated through, 3 to 4 minutes. Serve warm.

CAMBODIAN STIR-FRIED NOODLES
K'tieu Cha

SERVES 4

3 tablespoons vegetable oil

10 ounces rice noodles, soaked in warm water for
10–15 minutes and drained

⅓ cup mushroom soy sauce

About ¼ cup water or chicken broth

1 pound mung bean sprouts

¼ pound Chinese chives or scallions, cut into
2-inch pieces

1 cup peanuts, roasted and coarsely ground

Dipping Sauce for Spring Rolls (page 49)

Thinly sliced bird's eye chilies

In a large skillet or wok, heat the oil over high heat. Add the noodles and soy sauce, mixing thoroughly, and stir-fry for about 3 minutes, adding the water or broth 1 tablespoon at a time as necessary to keep the noodles from sticking.

Add half of the bean sprouts and half of the chives or scallions and stir-fry for 2 minutes. Remove from heat and transfer the noodles to individual bowls. Divide the remaining bean sprouts and chives or scallions among the bowls, adding a handful of peanuts to each. Pour the dipping sauce over all and top with chilies to taste. Toss and serve.

Khmers have this simple, delicious meatless dish for breakfast all the time, as well as for snacks, and you can find it everywhere. When I was little, vendors sold it from carts across the street from my primary school. My mother would never give us money to buy street food, so one afternoon, when she was napping, I stole some of her coins and had one of the servants buy me some stir-fried noodles — they tasted so fantastic that I had trouble feeling guilty. Years later, when my brothers and sisters were telling childhood stories, it came out that every one of us had done exactly the same thing — my poor mother, but, oh, that wonderful *K'tieu Cha*.

RICE NOODLES WITH GREEN SAUCE
Nom Banchok Somlah Khmer

SERVES 4

1–1½ pounds rice stick noodles, soaked in warm
    water for 10–15 minutes and drained

PASTE

1 stalk lemongrass, thinly sliced (include plenty of
    the green leaves, for color)
4 garlic cloves, coarsely chopped
1 medium shallot, coarsely chopped
8 kaffir lime leaves, deveined
2 teaspoons peeled, coarsely chopped galangal
2 pieces rhizome, each about 2½ inches long
¼ teaspoon turmeric
⅔ cup water

8 cups chicken broth
¾ pound catfish or tilapia fillets
2 tablespoons *prahok* juice (optional)
3 tablespoons fish sauce, plus more for serving
2 teaspoons salt
½ pound mung bean sprouts
1 pound English cucumber, julienned
¼ pound string beans, cut into ¼-inch pieces
¼ pound banana blossoms, thinly sliced and soaked
    in water with lime juice to keep from darkening
    (optional)
Thinly sliced green bird's eye chilies

Cambodian people reach chopsticks into this hearty noodle dish at breakfast, throughout the day for snacks or even in the middle of the night. It's usually served alone as a complete meal, and the noodles are cooked and arranged in tidy bundles on a platter so it's easy for people to get at them when they want more. The sauce gets its lovely green shade from lemongrass leaves, and in the northeast of Cambodia, where cooks tend to add coconut milk, it looks almost like a cream of spinach soup. My grandmother insisted on having these noodles every day for breakfast.

Bring a large pot of water to a boil. Add the noodles, turn off the heat and let sit for 15 minutes. Drain, rinse under cold water and drain again. Loop handfuls of the cooked noodles into bundles 8 to 10 inches long and place them on a platter.

To make the paste: Blend all the ingredients in a blender until smooth, 2 to 3 minutes. Set aside.

Bring the chicken broth to a boil in a large pot. Add the fish, lower the heat and simmer until tender, about 10 minutes.

When the fish is cooked, use a slotted spoon to transfer it to a small bowl (keep the broth on a low simmer), and break the fillets apart with a fork. Add the paste to the fish and blend well, stirring a couple tablespoons of the simmering broth into the fish-paste mixture until smooth. Stir the mixture back into the broth. Add the *prahok* juice (if using), fish sauce and salt. Return the broth to a boil, then remove from the heat.

Meanwhile, arrange the prepared vegetables on a platter and set out on the table with the platter of noodles. To serve, put handfuls of the vegetables in the bottom of each individual serving bowl and cover with a bundle of noodles, then broth. Serve with sliced green chilies and fish sauce on the side. Mix well just before eating.

NOODLES WITH RED SAUCE AND COCONUT
Nom Banchok Namya

SERVES 4

1–1½ pounds rice stick noodles, soaked in warm
    water for 10–15 minutes and drained

PASTE

3 dried New Mexico chilies, soaked, seeded and
    deveined

1 medium shallot, coarsely chopped

5 garlic cloves, coarsely chopped

2 tablespoons sliced lemongrass

2 pieces rhizome, each about 2 inches long

2 tablespoons peeled, coarsely chopped galangal

10 kaffir lime leaves, deveined

¼ teaspoon turmeric

1 tablespoon chopped fresh cilantro stems

⅔ cup water

3 cups chicken broth

¾ pound catfish or other firm white freshwater fish
    fillets, such as tilapia

2 tablespoons *prahok* juice (optional)

¼ cup vegetable oil

2¼ cups unsweetened coconut milk

5 tablespoons sugar

3 tablespoons fish sauce, plus more for serving

2½ teaspoons salt

8 kaffir lime leaves, deveined

4 cups water

⅛ teaspoon turmeric

¼ pound Chinese or regular watercress, cut into
    ¼-inch pieces

Rich with a sauce of coconut milk and a bright red chili paste, these noodles are lightened by crisp green vegetables and the tart lime juice. In the markets in Cambodia, you can buy cooked noodles in circular bundles called *chavai* and choose any kind of sauce to accompany them. This one was always one of my daughters' favorites. Most Cambodians would use only coconut milk for the sauce, but I add chicken broth as well to make it a little lighter; it also contributes flavor. See the photograph on page 217.

¼ pound Asian long beans (or regular string
    beans), cut into ¼-inch pieces
¼ pound mung bean sprouts
½ cup loosely packed fresh mint leaves
½ cup loosely packed fresh basil leaves
Lime wedges
Thinly sliced bird's eye chilies

Bring a large pot of water to a boil. Add the noodles, turn off the heat and let sit for 15 minutes. Drain, rinse under cold water and drain again. Loop handfuls of the cooked noodles into bundles 8 to 10 inches long, and place them on a platter.

TO MAKE THE PASTE: Blend all the ingredients in a blender until smooth, 2 to 3 minutes. Set aside.

Bring the chicken broth to a boil in a medium pot. Add the fish, lower the heat and simmer until tender, about 10 minutes. Add the *prahok* juice (if using) to the broth. Using a slotted spoon, transfer the fish to a small bowl (keep the broth on a low simmer), and break apart with a fork. Add the paste and blend well. Set aside.

In a large pot, heat the oil over medium-high heat. Add ½ cup of the coconut milk and cook, stirring, until the oil separates from the milk, about 2 minutes. Stir in the fish-paste mixture and cook to develop the flavors, 2 to 3 minutes. Add the broth and the remaining 1¾ cups coconut milk, along with the sugar, fish sauce, salt and kaffir lime leaves. Bring to a boil and cook for another 5 minutes.

Meanwhile, bring the water and turmeric to a boil in a medium saucepan. One vegetable at a time, blanch the watercress, beans and, if you like, the mung bean sprouts, by dipping them into the boiling water for a few seconds. Remove with a slotted spoon, drain and rinse with cold water. Arrange the vegetables and sprouts on a platter with the herbs and put out with the platter of noodles.

To serve, put handfuls of the vegetables in the bottom of each individual serving bowl, cover with a bundle of noodles and pour the broth over all. Serve with lime wedges, sliced bird's eye chilies and fish sauce on the side. Mix well before eating.

RICE NOODLES WITH FISH BALLS
Nom Banchok Sao Nam

SERVES 4

The sauce for these noodles combines mild fish balls with sweet rich coconut milk and sharp young ginger and pineapple in an intriguing and sumptuous way. Regular ginger is sharper than young ginger, so if you use it, reduce the amount to ½ cup. This recipe is something special that I want to leave to the younger generation of Cambodians, a dish that not too many of them would otherwise have known.

1–1½ pounds rice stick noodles, soaked in warm water for 10–15 minutes and drained
1 teaspoon salt
¾ cup peeled, finely julienned young ginger (about 3 ounces)

DRESSING
5 tablespoons fish sauce
2 tablespoons lime juice
¼ cup sugar
4 garlic cloves, smashed and finely chopped

1¼ cups unsweetened coconut milk
¾ pound Asian fish balls or ½ pound catfish fillets, cut into 1-inch cubes
3 large shallots, very thinly sliced
1 medium-sized ripe pineapple, peeled, cored and julienned
1 cup peanuts, roasted and coarsely ground
Cilantro sprigs, for garnish

Bring a large pot of water to a boil. Add the noodles, turn off the heat and let sit for 15 minutes. Drain, rinse under cold water and drain again. Loop handfuls of the cooked noodles into bundles 8 to 10 inches long and place them on a platter.

In a small bowl, add the salt to the ginger and let sit for a few minutes to neutralize the heat of the ginger somewhat. Rinse and drain, squeezing any extra water out with your hands. Set aside.

TO MAKE THE DRESSING: In a small bowl, mix all the ingredients together, stirring until the sugar dissolves. Set aside.

In a small saucepan over medium-high heat, bring the coconut milk to a boil. Add the fish balls or catfish cubes, lower the heat and simmer for 2 to 3 minutes, until the fish balls are heated through or the catfish is cooked.

Meanwhile, mix the prepared ginger, shallots and pineapple together in a serving bowl.

To serve, place some of the pineapple mixture in each individual bowl, add a bundle of noodles and spoon over some fish with coconut milk. Sprinkle with the peanuts, garnish with cilantro and splash with dressing to taste.

COOL RICE NOODLES WITH DRIED SHRIMP, COCONUT MILK AND HERBS
Nom Banchok Kampot

SERVES 4

I first tasted this noodle dish with its tasty shrimp topping at a food stall in the market at Kampot in the south of Cambodia, and I had to work hard to get the vendor to give me his recipe. The key to the dish is the quality of the dried shrimp, which should be a rich pinkish color and have a sweet, not salty, taste. Cambodians eat these noodles as a snack at any time of day.

1½ pounds rice stick noodles, soaked in warm water for 10–15 minutes and drained
2½ ounces dried shrimp, soaked in hot water to cover for 20 minutes, or until soft, and drained
½ cup unsweetened coconut milk
½ pound mung bean sprouts
½ English cucumber, julienned
1 cup loosely packed fresh mint leaves
1 cup loosely packed fresh basil leaves
3–4 leaves green leaf lettuce, cut crosswise into ½-inch-wide strips
1¼ cups Dressing for Noodles (opposite)

Bring a large pot of water to a boil. Add the soaked noodles, return to a boil and turn off the heat. Let stand for 15 minutes. Drain, rinse under cold water and drain again. Set aside.

Pound the soaked shrimp with a mortar and pestle or grind them in a mini-chop, pulsing three or four times to produce a range of textures, from powder to nearly whole.

Heat the coconut milk in a small saucepan over medium heat. Let cool slightly.

Divide the bean sprouts, cucumber, mint, basil and lettuce among four bowls. Top with the noodles and sprinkle with the ground shrimp. Drizzle each serving with the coconut milk and dressing to taste. Toss well and serve immediately.

DRESSING FOR NOODLES
Tuk Trey

MAKES ABOUT 1½ CUPS

1 cup water

¼ cup sugar

4 teaspoons white vinegar

¼ cup fish sauce

½ teaspoon salt

2 garlic cloves, finely chopped

In a small saucepan, bring the water to a boil and add the sugar, stirring to dissolve. Allow to cool. Stir in the remaining ingredients.

PORK AND SHRIMP NOODLES
K'tieu Cha Kroeung

SERVES 4

A well-seasoned sauce with pork and shrimp coats these flat rice noodles, making a filling meal. When I want something quicker and lighter, I omit the pork and shrimp, and the dish is still satisfying. Even the strips of egg omelets for the garnish — which are a nice touch and very pretty — can be skipped.

PASTE

2 dried New Mexico chilies, soaked, seeded, and deveined
6 garlic cloves
1 medium shallot
1 cup water

OMELETS

1 teaspoon vegetable oil
4 large eggs, beaten

¼ cup vegetable oil
½ pound pork loin, cut into pieces 2 inches long, 2 inches wide and ¼ inch thick
3 tablespoons soy sauce, plus more for serving
3 tablespoons fish sauce
1½ tablespoons sugar
¼ pound large shrimp, peeled, deveined and cut in half lengthwise down the back
1 small bird's eye chili, seeds removed (to make it less fiery)
¾ pound rice noodles, soaked in warm water for 10–15 minutes and drained
½ pound mung bean sprouts
¼ pound Chinese chives or scallions, cut into 2-inch pieces

TO MAKE THE PASTE: Blend all the ingredients in a blender until smooth, 2 to 3 minutes. Set aside.

TO MAKE THE OMELETS: Heat the oil in a small nonstick skillet over medium-high heat and add ¼ cup of the eggs, swirling to coat the bottom of the pan evenly. When the egg is set in the bottom of the pan, flip to cook the second side; the whole process should take about 1 minute. Cook the remaining eggs, ¼ cup at a time, in the same fashion, stacking the cooked omelets. Thinly slice the stacked omelets and set aside.

Heat the oil in a large skillet over high heat, add the paste and cook for about 1 minute. Stir in the pork, soy sauce, fish sauce and sugar. Add the shrimp and chili and cook, stirring, until the shrimp are opaque, 2 to 3 minutes.

Fold in the noodles, lower the heat to medium and cook for 4 to 5 minutes, mixing the noodles and sauce together (chopsticks are very good for drawing the noodles up from the bottom of the pan). If the sauce is too dry, add a little water, a tablespoon at a time.

Add the sprouts and chives or scallions to the noodle mixture and mix thoroughly. Continue to cook for another 2 to 3 minutes; the vegetables should still be slightly crisp.

Put the noodles out on a platter or individual plates and top with the strips of omelets. Serve with soy sauce.

SALADS

FRESH VEGETABLES AND FRUITS ARE ABUNDANT in Cambodian cuisine, and nowhere are they more central than in salads. In many of the recipes that follow, cucumbers and tomatoes, cabbage and carrots, onions and peppers, and bean sprouts and banana blossoms are all celebrated for their distinctive textures, colors, flavors and the intriguing ways in which they can be combined.

But salads are hardly just fruit-and-vegetable affairs, and, indeed, the whole notion of a vegetable side dish is conspicuously absent from the Cambodian culinary repertoire. Instead, a salad is composed of lots of fresh vegetables and fruits flavored with small quantities of meat and fish, brightened with mint and basil and tossed with a dressing of fish sauce, garlic, sugar and lime juice. Noodles appear occasionally, providing additional texture, and ground roasted peanuts and dried shrimp are regular features.

In a Cambodian meal, a salad is presented as one of several entrees, but in the American context, it can be interpreted in a number of different ways. Similar to a chef's salad, it makes a satisfying light meal, especially with rice—Provincial Beef Salad being an outstanding example. In other cases, you can easily omit the meat and serve the salad as a side dish; at The Elephant Walk, the popular Cambodian Cabbage Salad is often requested meatless.

DRESSING FOR SALAD
Tuk Trey

MAKES ABOUT 1¼ CUPS

¼ cup water
½ cup sugar
1 garlic clove
1 small shallot
½ cup fish sauce
5 teaspoons fresh lime juice
2 teaspoons salt

In a small saucepan, bring the water to a boil and add the sugar, stirring to dissolve. Set aside and allow to cool.

Pound the garlic and shallot into small pieces with a mortar and pestle or grind in a mini-chop. Stir into the sugar water, then add the remaining ingredients.

VEGETARIAN SALAD DRESSING
Tuk Trey

MAKES ABOUT 1½ CUPS

5½ tablespoons sugar
1½ cups water
3½ teaspoons salt
2½ tablespoons vinegar
1½ teaspoons finely chopped garlic
2 teaspoons mushroom soy sauce (optional)

Heat 2 tablespoons of the sugar with 1 teaspoon of the water in a small saucepan over medium-high heat. Bring to a boil, stirring to dissolve the sugar, then cook without stirring until it caramelizes, 2½ to 3 minutes. Add the remaining water and remaining 3½ tablespoons sugar and the salt, stirring to dissolve. Let cool, then add the vinegar and garlic.

A variation lets you bypass the caramelizing process: bring the water to a boil and add the sugar and salt, stirring to dissolve. Allow to cool. Add the remaining ingredients, along with 2 teaspoons mushroom soy sauce for color and flavor.

TOMATO SALAD
Nyuom Peng Pah
Serves 4

4 cups water

1 large whole chicken breast (about ¾ pound)

1 pound plum tomatoes (about 8), very thinly sliced

½ English cucumber, thinly sliced

½ cup loosely packed fresh mint leaves

½ cup loosely packed fresh basil leaves

⅓ cup Dressing for Salad (page 227) or Vegetarian
    Dressing (opposite page)

Thinly sliced bird's eye chilies

½ cup peanuts, roasted and coarsely ground

In a medium saucepan, bring the water to a boil and add the chicken breast. Return to a boil, reduce the heat to low and simmer for 10 to 15 minutes, or until the chicken is tender. Remove the chicken from the pan and allow it to cool slightly, then shred the meat with your fingers.

In a large salad bowl, combine the tomatoes, cucumber, mint and basil. Add the dressing and chilies to taste. Sprinkle with the peanuts. Toss and serve immediately.

Mint and basil are a popular combination in Cambodian cuisine, and the herbs make this tomato salad sparkle. Peanuts punctuate the dish without dominating. Using a chicken breast is particularly convenient, but in Cambodia, people might have slices of pork, whole shrimp and sliced hard-boiled eggs instead of the chicken or along with it. They might also sprinkle shredded dried shrimp over the top. To make this meal vegetarian, simply omit the chicken and choose Vegetarian Dressing.

CAMBODIAN CABBAGE SALAD
Salade Cambodgienne

SERVES 4

This cabbage salad has all the crisp freshness of a summer coleslaw, but the presence of chicken makes it more substantial, and the unmistakable combination of basil and mint, peanuts and a fish-sauce dressing marks it as Cambodian. We use many different Chinese greens in Khmer cooking — including bok choy and mustard greens — but the green cabbage in this salad is traditional. *Salade Cambodgienne* is almost a national dish.

4 cups water
1 large whole chicken breast (about ¾ pound)
1 head cabbage (about 2 pounds), cut in half and thinly sliced
1 cup shredded carrots
½ large onion, thinly sliced
½ red bell pepper, thinly sliced
½ cup loosely packed fresh mint leaves
½ cup loosely packed fresh basil leaves
½ cup peanuts, roasted and coarsely ground
⅓ cup Dressing for Salad (page 227)
Cilantro sprigs, for garnish

In a medium saucepan, bring the water to a boil, add the chicken breast and return to a boil. Reduce the heat and simmer for 10 to 15 minutes, until the meat is tender. Remove the chicken from the pan and let cool slightly, then shred the meat with your fingers.

In a large salad bowl toss all of the vegetables and herbs together with the chicken. Setting aside a handful for garnish, mix in the peanuts. Add the dressing and toss. Sprinkle with the remaining peanuts and garnish with cilantro. Serve immediately.

BANANA BLOSSOM SALAD
Nyuom Traiyong Chaek

SERVES 4

1 banana blossom (1–1½ pounds)

2 tablespoons fresh lemon juice

4 cups water

1 large whole chicken breast (about ¾ pound)

1 cup loosely packed fresh mint leaves,

1 cup loosely packed fresh basil leaves

½ pound mung bean sprouts

½ small red bell pepper, thinly sliced

½ cup peanuts, roasted and coarsely ground

⅓ cup Dressing for Salad (page 227)

Remove the tough outer leaves of the banana blossom and discard them, along with the undeveloped "baby" bananas inside. Carefully pull away the next several layers of leaves, regularly cutting into the stem to make it easier to break them off (the aim is to keep the leaves whole, if possible). Lay several leaves on top of one another and slice the leaves crosswise into ⅛-inch-wide strips. To keep the leaves from turning black, immediately place them in a large bowl with the lemon juice and water to cover, turning occasionally.

Continue in this fashion, releasing the leaves, discarding the undeveloped bananas and cutting the leaves into strips, until you reach the heart at the center. Cut it in half lengthwise, remove as many of the babies as possible, and slice the remaining leaves crosswise about ¼ inch thick.

In a medium saucepan, bring the 4 cups of water to a boil. Add the chicken breast, return to a boil, reduce the heat and simmer for 10 to 15 minutes, until the meat is tender.

The star ingredient of this fresh, bright salad is the banana blossom, whose lovely purple ringlets and mild, slightly nutty flavor blend beautifully with other aromatic herbs and vegetables, chicken and roasted peanuts. Except for the rows of banana "babies" hiding inside each leaf, the banana blossom is a lot like an uncooked artichoke, including the tendency for its leaves to darken when they've been cut. To show off this salad to best advantage, serve with rice and simply grilled chicken. See the photograph on page 233.

Remove the chicken from the pan and let cool slightly, then shred the meat with your fingers.

In a large salad bowl, toss all of the vegetables and herbs together with the chicken. Setting aside a handful for garnish, mix in the ground peanuts. Add the dressing and toss. Sprinkle with the remaining peanuts and serve immediately.

CLASSIC CUCUMBER SALAD
Nyuom Trausak

SERVES 4

This is a classic Khmer
salad, in which rice noodles
are flavored by pork and
shrimp and refreshed by
mint and cucumber. I
love eating this salad
all by itself.

1 ounce rice stick noodles, soaked in warm water for
 10–15 minutes and drained
4 cups water
½ pound pork tenderloin or fresh ham
¼ cup dried shrimp, soaked in warm water for 10
 minutes and drained
1 large English cucumber, thinly sliced
1 small shallot, thinly sliced
½ scallion, thinly sliced
¼ red bell pepper, julienned
1 cup loosely packed fresh mint leaves
1 cup loosely packed fresh basil leaves
⅓ cup Dressing for Salad (page 227)

Bring a medium saucepan of water to a boil and add the
noodles. Turn off the heat and let the noodles sit for 15 minutes. Drain, rinse under cold water and drain again. Set aside.

In a medium saucepan, bring the 4 cups water to a boil
and add the pork. Return to a boil, reduce the heat to low and
simmer for 30 minutes, or until tender. Remove from heat
and drain.

Pound the soaked shrimp with a mortar and pestle or
grind in a mini-chop for 5 to 10 seconds, until well shredded.
Julienne the pork into ¼-inch-thick pieces.

In large bowls, toss the noodles, shrimp and pork with
the cucumber, shallot, scallion, red pepper and herbs. Toss
with the dressing and serve immediately.

PINEAPPLE SALAD
Nyuom M'noa

SERVES 4

3 cups water

½ pound pork tenderloin or fresh ham

1 medium-sized firm green pineapple (about
  1½–2 pounds), peeled, sliced and julienned

2 large shallots, very thinly sliced

½ cup loosely packed fresh mint leaves

½ cup loosely packed fresh basil leaves

2 tablespoons fresh lime juice

4 teaspoons fish sauce

4 teaspoons sugar

1 teaspoon salt

¼ red bell pepper, julienned

Bring the water to a boil in a medium saucepan. Add the pork and simmer for 30 minutes, or until cooked through; drain.

Julienne the pork into ¼-inch-thick pieces. In a serving bowl, combine the pork with the pineapple, shallots, mint and basil.

In a small bowl, mix the lime juice, fish sauce, sugar and salt, stirring to dissolve the sugar, and add to the pork. Toss well, garnish with red pepper and serve.

This lively pineapple salad is perfect made with pork, but it's also terrific with chicken (in the same quantity). You can add shrimp (¼ pound, cut into bite-sized pieces and simmered for 2 minutes) to either one. An underripe pineapple provides a nice acidic counterpoint to any of these flavors, to the herbs and to the slightly sweet dressing. For a fancier presentation, try serving the salad in the pineapple. Cut the pineapple in half lengthwise and scoop out the fruit, then core and slice it. This dish goes well with a rich entree like Beef with Eggplant in Coconut Milk (page 117) or Royal Catfish Enrobed with Coconut Milk and Lemongrass (page 163), but it also shines with simple grilled fish or meats.

POMELO SALAD
Nyuom Kroit T'long

SERVES 4

The combination of pork and pomelo (first cousin to the grapefruit) might sound strange at first, but this salad is one of the liveliest in the Khmer repertoire. The pork adds some underlying richness, but it is the citrusy taste of the pomelo, laced with coconut, that is the star. Pomelo is perfect for this dish because of its firm texture, which allows the fruit to be separated into individual teardrop-shaped pockets of juice, and because guests tend to appreciate the extra care given to such preparations, I like to serve this salad for company. In part because of its slightly sharp flavor, Pomelo Salad is particularly excellent with rice.

3 cups water
½ pound pork tenderloin or fresh ham
2½ pounds pomelo (1–2)
½ cup freshly grated coconut or packaged
    unsweetened shredded coconut
2 large shallots, very thinly sliced
1 garlic clove, smashed and finely chopped
1 scallion, thinly sliced
5 teaspoons sugar
2 teaspoons fish sauce
1 teaspoon salt
Fresh lime juice, to taste (optional)

Bring the water to a boil in a medium saucepan. Add the pork and simmer for 30 minutes, or until cooked through; drain and set aside.

Meanwhile, prepare the pomelo by peeling it and separating into segments, then pulling off the membranes. Tease the flesh apart into small clumps or individual sacs and put into a medium serving bowl.

Toast the coconut in a small skillet over medium heat (or toast in the oven on a small baking sheet at 325°F), shaking and stirring regularly until evenly browned, 3 to 4 minutes. Allow to cool.

Julienne the pork into ¼-inch-thick slices. Add the pork to the pomelo, along with the cooled coconut, shallots, garlic and scallion. Sprinkle with the sugar, fish sauce and salt and toss well. (If the pomelo is very sweet and the overall effect lacks sharpness, adjust the flavors by adding up to 2 teaspoons lime juice to make it tarter.) Serve immediately.

GREEN PAPAYA SALAD
Nyuom L'hong

SERVES 6

2 pounds green papaya (1–2), peeled, cut in half and
    white seed area removed

½ cup dried shrimp, soaked in warm water for
    10 minutes and drained

2½ tablespoons tamarind juice

2 tablespoons *prahok* juice (optional)

3 tablespoons fish powder

4 garlic cloves, smashed and finely chopped

1 large shallot, very thinly sliced

1 tablespoon sugar

½ teaspoon salt

¼ cup sliced scallions

¼ cup loosely packed fresh mint leaves

¼ cup loosely packed fresh basil leaves

1 tablespoon fresh lime juice

Grate the papaya, to yield about 6 cups (a mandoline or the grating attachment on a food processor simplifies this step considerably).

Pound the shrimp with a mortar and pestle or grind in a mini-chop for 5 to 10 seconds.

In a serving bowl, combine the tamarind juice, *prahok* juice (if using), fish powder, garlic, shallot, sugar and salt, stirring well. Add the papaya and dried shrimp. Sprinkle with the scallions, mint, basil and lime juice, toss lightly and serve.

What makes this salad so interesting are all the flavors that are mixed with the papaya: the garlic, tamarind and shrimp and—for those who want it—the *prahok*. The result is a kind of smoky flavor, heavier than that of most of the other salads in this chapter, and one that is more complex. When I was little, I loved to have a big bowl of this salad in the middle of the afternoon with lots of extra *prahok* to liven it up and tiny freshwater shrimp sprinkled on top. To approximate the firm, crunchy texture and mild flavor of the green papaya, you could also use chayote or jicama.

BEAN THREAD NOODLE SALAD
Nyuom Mee Souah

SERVES 4

6 cups water

3–4 ounces bean thread noodles, soaked in warm
  water for 10–15 minutes and drained

¼ cup dried shrimp, soaked in warm water for
  10 minutes and drained (optional)

½ pound pork tenderloin or fresh ham

½ English cucumber, julienned

¼ red bell pepper, julienned

½ pound mung bean sprouts

1 cup loosely packed fresh mint leaves

1 cup loosely packed fresh basil leaves

½ cup peanuts, roasted and finely ground

Dressing for Salad (page 227)

A Cambodian cook at The Elephant Walk introduced me only recently to this light yet filling salad. It tastes great with chicken breast or shrimp, as well as with pork, and you can add more of anything else that you like.

In a large pot, bring the water to a boil. Meanwhile, cut the bean thread noodles with scissors into pieces 2 to 3 inches long. Put the noodles in a strainer and dip into the boiling water for about 10 seconds, or until they are soft but not mushy. Rinse under cold running water and drain.

Pound the shrimp with a mortar and pestle or grind briefly in a mini-chop for 5 to 10 seconds to produce a range of textures, from powdery to nearly whole.

Bring a medium saucepan of water to a boil. Add the pork, reduce the heat to low and simmer for 30 minutes, or until cooked through. Drain and allow to cool slightly. Cut into ¼-inch-thick julienne strips.

Put the pork, cucumber, red pepper, bean sprouts, mint, basil and noodles in a large serving bowl. Sprinkle with the shrimp and the ground peanuts, saving some of peanuts for the garnish. Toss thoroughly. Add enough dressing to moisten the salad and toss again. Sprinkle with the remaining peanuts and serve.

PROVINCIAL BEEF SALAD
Salat Kompong Ch'hnang

SERVES 4

I often make this lettuce
and tomato salad with
slices of beef and hard-
boiled eggs for my
husband, Ken, because it's
so simple. You can see the
French influence in the
salad, especially in the use
of the vinaigrette, and my
mother used to prepare it
all the time—although my
father wouldn't always eat
it because it wasn't fancy
enough. You can adjust all
the amounts to suit your
own taste; for instance, I
like to use extra hard-
boiled eggs and to serve
the salad as a complete
meal with rice.

½ cup plus 1 tablespoon vegetable oil
¾ pound boneless sirloin steak or top round, cut
    into 1½-inch cubes, then sliced thinly across the
    grain
1 large onion, thinly sliced lengthwise
2½ teaspoons salt
½ teaspoon freshly ground pepper
2 heads green leaf lettuce (about 1 pound), separated
    into leaves, washed and drained
3 plum tomatoes (about ½ pound), very thinly
    sliced
2 hard-boiled eggs, thinly sliced
3½ teaspoons balsamic or red wine vinegar
1½ teaspoons Dijon mustard

Heat 1 tablespoon of the oil in a large skillet over medium-high heat and cook the beef, stirring constantly, for about 2 minutes. Add half of the onion slices, 1 teaspoon of the salt and the pepper and continue stir-frying for another 2 minutes (the beef will be on the rare side; cook longer if you prefer). Set aside.

Tear the lettuce leaves into small pieces, removing the thick center ribs, and arrange on a platter. Top with the sliced tomatoes and eggs. Mix the remaining ½ cup oil with the vinegar, mustard and the remaining 1½ teaspoons salt. Toss the beef and the remaining onions with the dressing, then distribute evenly on the platter.

LIME-MARINATED BEEF WITH BEAN SPROUTS AND MINT
Pleah Saiko

SERVES 4

¾ cup fresh lime juice (3–4 limes)

5 tablespoons sugar

1 stalk lemongrass, very thinly sliced

2 garlic cloves, smashed and finely chopped

1 pound boneless top round, sliced as thinly as
possible against the grain

¼ cup fish sauce

¼ cup water

1½ tablespoons *prahok* juice (optional)

1 shallot, thinly sliced

1 cup mung bean sprouts

½ cup loosely packed fresh mint leaves

½ cup loosely packed fresh basil leaves

¼ cup peanuts, roasted and coarsely ground

In this salad, raw beef is marinated in lime juice and then tossed with mung bean sprouts, fresh herbs and chopped peanuts. The result is a remarkably light, fresh-tasting meal that is at the same time filling. The addition of the *prahok* juice makes this distinctively Cambodian, but even without it, the salad is delicious. I fear that this recipe has been lost to the younger generation, and I would like to help restore it. See the photograph on page 243.

Combine ¼ cup of the lime juice with 1 tablespoon of the sugar, the lemongrass and half of the garlic in a medium bowl. Mix well, then add the beef, tossing to coat evenly, and set aside to marinate at room temperature for 25 to 30 minutes.

Meanwhile, combine the fish sauce, water, *prahok* juice (if using) and the remaining ¼ cup sugar in a small bowl. Mix until the sugar dissolves completely, then add the remaining ½ cup lime juice, shallot and the remaining garlic. Set aside.

Drain the beef, pressing gently with your hands to remove as much liquid as possible. Wipe out the bowl. Return the beef to the bowl and add the bean sprouts, mint, basil and half the ground peanuts. Toss well, add the dressing and toss again, then transfer to a platter. Garnish the salad with the remaining peanuts and serve.

FISH SALAD WITH LIME AND CRUNCHY VEGETABLES
Pleah Trey

SERVES 4

Asian seviche is a perfect example of how salty and sweet, cured and fresh flavors are balanced in Khmer cuisine. This recipe takes some work, but its results are classically Khmer. For variety, I sometimes add lobster instead of, or in addition to, the fish, and my daughter Nadsa likes to add julienned jicama to give the salad additional crunch and sweetness. Because the fish is not cooked, be sure it is absolutely fresh.

1¼ pounds very fresh catfish, sea bass or tilapia fillets

½ cup plus 2 tablespoons fresh lime juice (about 3 limes)

3 teaspoons salt

5 ¼-inch-thick slices peeled galangal

7 garlic cloves, sliced

2 large shallots, coarsely chopped

6 tablespoons sugar

5 tablespoons fish sauce

5 tablespoons white vinegar

2 tablespoons *prahok* juice (optional)

1 medium head green leaf lettuce, separated, washed, drained and torn into pieces 2–3 inches long

½ pound bean sprouts

1½ cups loosely packed fresh mint leaves

1½ cups loosely packed fresh basil leaves

½ English cucumber, julienned

½ small onion, very thinly sliced

½ cup peeled, julienned jicama (optional)

¼ red bell pepper, julienned

1 stalk lemongrass, very thinly sliced

½ cup peanuts, roasted and coarsely ground

Thinly sliced bird's eye chilies

Cut the fillets lengthwise in half, then slice crosswise into ⅛-inch-wide pieces. Place ½ cup of the lime juice and 2 teaspoons of the salt in a medium bowl, then add the fish, stirring well to coat. Set aside to marinate for at least 30 minutes.

Squeeze out as much of the liquid from the fish as possible with your fingers (there should be about 1 cup) and reserve it for the sauce. Set the fish aside.

Heat a small skillet over high heat. Sear the galangal, pressing and turning occasionally, until it is well browned, about 3 minutes. Put the galangal, garlic, shallots and the reserved lime-fish juice in a blender and blend for 1 to 2 minutes, until smooth.

Pour the liquid into a saucepan and set over medium-high heat, stirring as you add the sugar, fish sauce, vinegar, the remaining 2 tablespoons lime juice, the remaining teaspoon salt and *prahok* juice (if using). Cook, stirring occasionally, until the flavors are well blended, 7 to 8 minutes. Remove from the heat and allow to cool.

In a large bowl, toss together the lettuce, bean sprouts, mint, basil, cucumber, onion, jicama (if using), red pepper and lemongrass. Arrange on a platter. Shredding the fish with your fingers, distribute it evenly over the vegetables. Pour the sauce over the top and sprinkle with the roasted peanuts. Serve with bird's eye chilies.

FRESH VEGETABLES WITH DIPPING SAUCE
Prahok K'tih

SERVES 4

1 tablespoon vegetable oil
⅓ cup pea eggplant or cubed (½ inch) regular
    eggplant

PASTE

1 dried New Mexico chili, soaked, seeded and
    deveined
2 garlic cloves, coarsely chopped
1 large shallot, coarsely chopped
1 cup water

¼ cup vegetable oil
¾ pound ground pork
Up to ½ cup *prahok* juice (optional)
½ cup tamarind juice
½ cup unsweetened coconut milk
5 tablespoons sugar
2 teaspoons salt
6 small Asian eggplant or 1 large regular eggplant
    (about ½ pound)
1 English cucumber, cut lengthwise in half and
    thinly sliced
½ small head cabbage, cut into 1-inch chunks
4-6 ounces string beans
Thinly sliced bird's eye chilies

Prahok K'tih is an artful, delicious way to enjoy a variety of vegetables raw, including eggplant and green beans. The rich dipping sauce, a nicely spiced combination of pork and coconut milk, is further seasoned with *prahok*, added in quantities to suit individual tastes. Particularly when you are just starting out with *prahok*—and I recommend trying it because I believe it can enrich your palate enormously—serve it with plenty of rice, which allows the flavors to expand and develop.

Heat the oil in a small pan and cook the eggplant over high heat, stirring, until well browned on all sides, 3 to 4 minutes. Set aside.

To make the paste: Blend the chili, garlic, shallot and water in a blender until smooth, about 1½ minutes. Set aside.

Heat the oil in a large skillet over medium-high heat and cook the pork for about 5 minutes, stirring occasionally to break apart the meat. Stir in the paste and continue cooking as you add the *prahok* juice (if using), tamarind juice, coconut milk, sugar and salt. Cook for another 10 minutes, until the flavors are thoroughly blended. Stir the pea eggplant or cubed eggplant into the pork mixture and cook for 5 minutes more, until heated through. Remove from the heat, allow to cool and transfer to a bowl.

Meanwhile, create eggplant "fans" from the Asian or regular eggplant by removing the stem and making a series of slices about ⅛ inch apart and three-quarters of the way through the flesh, from blossom to stem end. Bend the eggplant slightly to open the fan. (Soaking in cold water for 10 minutes will make it easier to open the eggplant.)

Arrange the raw eggplant, cucumber, cabbage and string beans on a platter and serve with the bowl of pork mixture as a dipping sauce, with chilies on the side for additional spicing.

PICKLES AND RELISHES

PICKLES AND RELISHES ARE INTENDED TO provide intensified bursts of flavor and tart highlights that complement the rest of the dishes making up the Cambodian meal. Generally salty as well as sour, and often with a lovely balancing of sweetness, these condiments add a crisp, crunchy texture. The jewel-like quality of Red Pepper Relish or the assorted shapes in Mixed Vegetable Pickles offer wonderful visual appeal at any table.

In Cambodia, the purpose of pickling vegetables and fruits is less to preserve them for extended lengths of time and more to sour them for short-term use. Produce is not cooked and canned as it is in this country but tends to be stored in a simple brine or vinegar and put out in the sun to ferment. In the summer in New England, I always put my pickles outside, but for the rest of the year, I place them next to the furnace (although any heat source will do). Once they have properly soured, the pickles should be refrigerated. Otherwise they will quickly lose their crunchiness.

Pickles and relishes go perfectly with grilled meats and fish and are natural accompaniments to rice. Roasted rice is sometimes added to a relish to give it a subtle, aromatic quality, but you can just as easily take these condiments in another direction, sparking them up with chilies. Most of the pickles and relishes included here will keep for a week or two in the refrigerator, but I have rarely had the opportunity to check the exact number of days because they disappear so quickly.

CUCUMBER PICKLES
Chrourk Trausak Khmer

MAKES 3 TO 4 PINTS

4 cups water

5 tablespoons salt

2 pounds cucumbers (preferably small pickling
cucumbers or gherkins), washed well but not
peeled

Bring the water to a boil in a medium saucepan and add the salt, stirring to dissolve. Remove from the heat.

Pack the cucumbers into sealable glass jars (clean mayonnaise jars are perfect). Leave small cucumbers whole and cut larger ones crosswise in half and slice them into spears. Pour the hot salted water over the cucumbers.

Leave the jars open until the liquid cools, then put on the lids and store in a warm place for 2 to 3 days (cool weather will lengthen the time by a day or two). The pickles are ready when the skin of the cucumbers turns an olive color and the liquid is sour but the cucumbers are still crunchy.

The pickles will keep in the refrigerator for about a week.

These crunchy sour pickles are great to make in the summertime when gardens overflow with cucumbers. Summer is the best time to pickle for another reason: the brighter sun and warmer air speed up the process considerably. Pickling cucumbers or gherkins work well in this recipe, but feel free to try other varieties that bear small fruit with few seeds. Cucumber pickles are terrific with any grilled meat or fish.

TOMATO RELISH
Chrourk Peng Pah

MAKES ABOUT 1½ CUPS

The green tomatoes in this relish provide tartness, crunch and color, but it's the garlic and roasted rice that make it special. Since the relish can be made quickly and doesn't require any fancy ingredients it is a perfect food for unexpected guests. I like it best with grilled fish and meats, and I add lots of the bird's eye chilies for an extra kick.

½ pound ripe but firm tomatoes, well washed
½ pound green tomatoes, well washed
7 garlic cloves, smashed and finely chopped
3 tablespoons white vinegar
2 tablespoons sugar
2 tablespoons roasted rice powder
1 tablespoon fish sauce
1 teaspoon salt
Thinly sliced bird's eye chilies

Cut the tomatoes in half and thinly slice. Place in a small bowl and add the garlic, vinegar, sugar, rice powder, fish sauce and salt, folding in gently so as not to completely break up the tomatoes. Serve with bird's eye chilies on the side.

PICKLED BEAN SPROUTS
Chrourk Samdaik

MAKES ABOUT 2 PINTS

2½ cups water

1½ tablespoons salt

¾ pound bean sprouts (about 5 cups), rinsed

¼ cup peeled, very thinly julienned ginger
(about 1 ounce)

———————

Bring the water to a boil in a small saucepan, and add the salt, stirring to dissolve. Set aside to cool.

In a large bowl, combine the bean sprouts and julienned ginger, then transfer to sealable jars (clean mayonnaise jars are perfect). Pack tightly and leave the top fifth of each jar empty. Fill the jars with the salt-water brine and seal. Store in a very warm place for 2 days, then refrigerate.

The bean sprouts will keep refrigerated for 1 to 2 weeks.

These are my favorite pickles. I love the light lemony flavor the bean sprouts take on after they soak for a couple of days. And because they are white, they make a dramatic appearance among other more colorful foods. Serve Pickled Bean Sprouts with rice and any kind of grilled meat and fish; the flavors and textures complement each other perfectly.

PICKLED BEAN SPROUTS WITH TOMATOES
Chrourk Samdaik Nung Peng Pah

MAKES ABOUT 2½ PINTS

2½ cups water
1½ tablespoons salt
¾ pound bean sprouts (about 5 cups)
2 tablespoons roasted rice powder
3 medium plum tomatoes, thinly sliced

This rural variation on Pickled Bean Sprouts includes tomatoes and roasted rice, which add extra tart and nutty flavors. When all the high-ranking officials in the Cambodian government were sent off to do manual labor in the countryside (a mini–cultural revolution, Khmer style), my husband, Ken, was introduced to these pickles by the peasants he worked with, who served them with freshly grilled fish.

Bring the water to a boil in a small saucepan and add the salt, stirring to dissolve. Set aside to cool.

In a large bowl, combine the bean sprouts, rice powder and sliced tomatoes, then transfer to sealable jars (clean mayonnaise jars are perfect). Pack tightly and leave the top fifth of each jar empty. Fill the jars with the salt-water brine and seal. Store in a very warm place for 2 days, then refrigerate.

The bean sprouts will keep refrigerated for 1 to 2 weeks.

RED PEPPER RELISH
Chrourk M'teh

MAKES ABOUT 2 CUPS

- 2 large red bell peppers (about 1 pound)
- 6 garlic cloves, thinly sliced
- 3 tablespoons white vinegar
- 3 tablespoons fish sauce
- 2 tablespoons sugar
- 1 teaspoon salt
- 1 cup julienned fresh or canned bamboo
  shoots (optional)

This brilliant red relish is a good match for grilled fish, especially catfish, and for broiled or barbecued meat. In Cambodia, people make the relish with boiled peppers, but I like them roasted: the smoky flavor is a great addition. Bamboo shoots, which are optional, add a nice crunch.

Preheat the oven to 400°F. Roast the red peppers on a baking sheet, turning occasionally, until they are well softened and slightly charred, 25 to 30 minutes. Seal in a plastic bag for 15 to 20 minutes to help loosen the skins. Peel, remove the seeds and finely chop the peppers (do not puree).

Place the peppers in a medium bowl and add the remaining ingredients and stir well. The relish keeps in the refrigerator for about a week.

MIXED VEGETABLE PICKLES
Chrourk Chamros

MAKES ABOUT 3 CUPS

As soon as you taste this medley of pickled vegetables, you'll wish you had made more. And its lively appearance only adds to the appeal. The crunchy carrots, cucumbers and cabbage are particularly well suited to one another, but feel free to experiment with other vegetables, including cauliflower and string beans, which you may like just as well. Serve with brochettes and other grilled foods.

2¼ cups water

3 tablespoons sugar

2 tablespoons white vinegar

2 teaspoons salt

½ pound cabbage, cut into 1½-inch chunks

½ pound cucumbers, washed well but not peeled, halved, seeded and cut into 1½-inch cubes

½ pound carrots, unpeeled, sliced on the diagonal ⅛ inch thick

4 garlic cloves, thinly sliced

2 tablespoons peeled, julienned ginger

Bring the water to a boil in a small saucepan, add the sugar, vinegar and salt and stir to dissolve. Remove from the heat and allow to cool.

Mix the vegetables together with the garlic and ginger and pack tightly into sealable jars (clean mayonnaise jars are perfect). Pour the liquid over the top, pressing down on the vegetables so that they are covered, and seal. Store overnight in a warm spot before serving.

These pickles will keep in the refrigerator for 1 to 2 weeks.

CUCUMBER RELISH
Chrourk Trausak

MAKES ABOUT 2½ CUPS

1 English cucumber or 1½ regular cucumbers
½ cup peeled, julienned ginger (about 2 ounces)
2 large shallots, thinly sliced
⅛ red bell pepper, thinly sliced
2 tablespoons white vinegar
1½ tablespoons sugar
1 tablespoon fish sauce
½ teaspoon salt
Thinly sliced bird's eye chilies, seeded if desired
    (optional)

This relish is the traditional accompaniment for Pork Brochettes with Shredded Coconut (page 58). When you eat these foods together, be sure to get some of each in every bite.

Remove the ends of the cucumber and, without peeling it, pierce the skin all over with a fork so that it will absorb the pickling flavors well. Slice as thin as possible, about ¹⁄₁₆ inch thick, so that the slices are almost translucent (you should have about 2½ cups).

Place the cucumber slices in a bowl and add the ginger, shallots, red pepper, vinegar, sugar, fish sauce and salt, mixing thoroughly. Serve immediately, as the pickles become watery quickly. You can add chili peppers, with or without seeds, to make these pickles nicely hot.

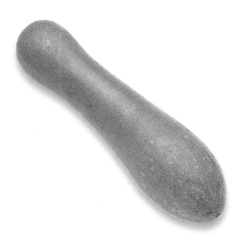

PICKLED BIRD'S EYE CHILIES
Chrourk M'teh K'mang

Some of my relatives in California grow their own bird's eye chilies, and when they have a particularly large harvest, they often put up some of them in this manner. Pickled Bird's Eye Chilies keep well in the refrigerator and can be used in place of fresh chilies, so it makes sense to buy a lot at once and pickle them if you don't have a ready supply.

2 cups water
½ teaspoon salt
1 or more cups bird's eye chilies, stemmed
    and washed well

Bring the water to a boil, add the salt and stir to dissolve. Set aside to cool.

Fill a jar with bird's eye chilies and cover with the cooled salt water. Allow the chilies to sit for 2 days before using. They will keep for at least 1 month in the refrigerator.

PICKLED MUSTARD GREENS
Chrourk Spey K'mao

MAKES 4 QUARTS

5½ cups water
3 tablespoons salt
1 teaspoon sugar
3 pounds mustard greens, stemmed and rinsed well

You can find pickled mustard greens in any Asian market, but this recipe allows you to make them yourself. I use them in soups and stir-fries and serve them with grilled chicken. They are very versatile.

Bring the water to a boil and add the salt and sugar, stirring to dissolve. Remove from the heat and set aside.

Shake off as much of the water from the mustard greens as possible and break the larger leaves in half along the center stem. Pack them tightly into a 4-quart container with a lid (or several smaller lidded containers). Pour the hot water over the top, pressing down on the greens as they soften, to fit snugly in the container(s).

When completely cool, cover the container(s) tightly and place in a warm place: during the summer, 3 days outside in strong sunlight is all that's needed; in the winter, 5 days near a heat source should do it. The greens are ready when they are olive-colored and their taste is sour.

The mustard greens keep refrigerated for up to 3 weeks.

DESSERTS

THE DESSERT COURSE IS NOT USUALLY PART OF A Cambodian meal. Instead, Cambodians tend to eat sweets as snacks, with great pleasure and appreciation. Many of these treats are made very simply, as in the case of Sweet Sliced Corn, which is nothing more than very thinly sliced corn kernels topped with honey and grated coconut, while others are quite elaborate, such as Sweet Mung Bean Rolls, tiny rolls of mung bean paste blended with coconut milk, dipped in egg yolk and cooked in a sugar syrup.

The majority of Cambodian sweets tend to feature a fairly limited number of ingredients. Grated coconut and sweetened coconut milk are central. Sticky rice and corn, both starchy, are common, and tapioca is often used as a thickener. Mung beans or black-eyed peas, cooked and mashed into a paste, provide similar kinds of textural backdrops for various fruits, which add interest, color and perfumed flavors.

As evidenced by some of the ingredients and techniques in the recipes that follow, Cambodian desserts have been influenced by other cuisines—for example, by the French in the case of Buttercup Egg Custard and by imperial Thai cooking with Golden Angel Hair—but they will probably appear mostly foreign to Western eyes. But when persuaded to try Sweet Pea and Coconut Pudding or Sweet Mung Bean Rolls, even the staunchest skeptics have become converts, and those who've experienced the elegant New Year's Rice Treats emerging from fragrant banana leaves have declared them nothing short of divine. Allow yourself to succumb.

SWEET SLICED CORN
Poat Chet

Making several passes with a very sharp knife (a mando-line makes this job easier), thinly slice steamed corn off the cob. Spread the corn out on a plate, drizzle with honey (or sprinkle with sugar) and serve with lots of freshly grated coconut on the top. Partly in memory of my father, and partly because there is such delicious honesty to the food, I always think of Sweet Sliced Corn as special.

My father, the gourmet, really ate only one dessert, and that was this very modest Sweet Sliced Corn.

CORN PUDDING
B'baw Poat

SERVES 4

3 ears corn
1½ tablespoons small Asian tapioca pearls
    or regular tapioca, rinsed
1 cup water
¾ cup unsweetened coconut milk
5 tablespoons sugar
¼ teaspoon salt

———————

With a very sharp knife, make several passes across the kernels of the corn until you're down to the bare cob, then scrape against the cob to get out the milky starch. (If using a mandoline or other scraper, pass the cob back and forth over the cutting blades several times.) You should have 2½ to 3 cups.

Place the tapioca in a large saucepan with the water and ½ cup of the coconut milk and bring to a boil, stirring occasionally. If using the small Asian tapioca pearls, add the corn kernels and juices now, reduce the heat to low and simmer until the tapioca starts to thicken and the corn is tender, about 15 minutes. Regular tapioca, which has larger pearls, requires more time to simmer; add the corn kernels during the last 15 minutes of cooking the tapioca, following the timing instructions on the package.

Stir in the sugar and salt and divide the pudding among four bowls. Spoon a tablespoon of the remaining coconut milk into the middle of each bowl. Serve warm.

NEW YEAR'S RICE TREATS
Nom N'sahm Chaek

MAKES ABOUT 10 ROLLS

1 cup unsweetened coconut milk, plus more for
  serving
1 teaspoon salt
1½ cups glutinous rice, soaked at least 2 hours or
  overnight (you should be able to split a grain
  easily with your fingernail), and drained
½ cup freshly grated coconut or packaged
  unsweetened shredded coconut
1 1-pound package frozen banana leaves
12 small Asian bananas or regular bananas (about
  1½ pounds)

Fill the bottom of a steamer with water and bring to a
boil.

Meanwhile, put the coconut milk and salt in a large
saucepan and bring to a boil over medium-high heat, stirring.
Stir in the rice and coconut. Reduce the heat to medium and
cook, stirring constantly, until the liquid has been absorbed
into the rice, 3 to 4 minutes. Press into the rice with a spoon:
the rice is done if it doesn't stick to the spoon.

Spread out the banana leaves on a work surface. Cut away
the tough vein and wipe the leaves clean. Cut the leaves
crosswise to produce a series of rectangles.

Place a banana leaf rectangle dark side
down on a work surface. Wetting your hands to
prevent the rice from sticking, press about ⅓ cup of
the cooked rice into a 5-inch circle in the middle of the leaf.
If you are using regular banana leaves, cut them to fit. Place a
banana in the middle of the rice (figure 1).

These wonderful rolls
made of sticky rice and
bananas are always served
during the celebration of
the Cambodian New Year.
The combination of a
luscious coconut flavor and
the subtle aroma of the
banana leaves makes the
rolls both a special snack
and a festive dessert. They
do require some advance
preparation, but you
can reduce the time
significantly if you use
aluminum foil to wrap
them, an alternative I was
forced to try when we lived
in France and couldn't get
banana leaves. See the
photograph on page 267.

FIGURE 1

FIGURE 2

FIGURE 3

Gently pull up the sides of the banana leaf to meet in the middle (figure 2), bringing the rice up to encase the banana, covering the ends by pinching the leaves together (figure 3).

Tightly roll the rice and banana up in the leaf as if rolling a cigarette (figure 4).

To seal, fold the ends of the banana leaf under on both sides (figure 5). Place the rolls in the steamer, folded side down, over boiling water, leaving room between them so the steam can penetrate. Cover and steam for about 25 minutes, or until the rice is completely translucent and the bananas are soft.

It is also possible to grill the rolls, which will add a smoky flavor. Instead of folding under the ends, use toothpicks to hold them closed and grill the rolls until the banana leaf wrapping is completely browned and the rice is translucent.

Serve on a platter warm or at room temperature, with coconut milk on the side. Before eating, unwrap the rolls, discard the banana leaves and slice the rolls crosswise into bite-sized pieces.

FIGURE 4   FIGURE 5

STICKY RICE WITH PALM FRUIT
B'baw T'noat

This Cambodian version of rice pudding is made with sticky rice and coconut milk. The palm fruit adds a sweet, slightly nutty flavor, with a soft texture. Served with additional coconut milk, *B'baw T'noat* is the perfect ending to a meal.

SERVES 4

1 cup water
⅔ cup glutinous rice, rinsed
3½ cups unsweetened coconut milk
1 cup sugar
½ teaspoon salt
1 can (20 ounces) palm fruit, drained and sliced

Combine the water, rice and 3 cups of the coconut milk in a large saucepan and bring to a boil over medium-high heat, stirring regularly. Reduce the heat to low and simmer, still stirring to keep the rice from sticking, until the rice begins to break down into a mush, about 35 minutes.

Add the sugar, salt and palm fruit and cook for another 10 minutes. Transfer to individual bowls, pour 2 tablespoons of the remaining coconut milk over each portion, and serve.

BANANAS IN SWEET COCONUT MILK
Chaek K'tih

SERVES 4

2 cups unsweetened coconut milk, plus more for
    serving

½ cup water

2 tablespoons small Asian tapioca pearls or regular
    tapioca, rinsed

12 small Asian bananas or 3–4 regular bananas
    (about 1½ pounds)

½ cup sugar

½ teaspoon salt

2 tablespoons dried split mung beans or sesame
    seeds

In this dish, sweet bananas are cooked in a thick, rich coconut milk sauce and topped with roasted mung beans or sesame seeds. You can find the small bananas for this dessert in any Asian market, and Hispanic groceries carry something very similar. If you need to, you can always use the regular bananas from the corner grocery store. See the photograph on page 271.

Put the 2 cups coconut milk and the water in a large saucepan and bring to a boil. Stir in the tapioca and bring back to a boil, then reduce the heat to low and simmer, stirring, until the tapioca becomes translucent and soft, 10 to 15 minutes for tiny pearls, longer for larger tapioca pearls.

Meanwhile, slice the bananas lengthwise in half, then cut crosswise in half; if using regular bananas, cut each half into thirds or quarters. Gently stirring, add the bananas, sugar and salt to the tapioca and cook for 10 minutes more. Remove from the heat.

While the bananas are cooking, put the dried mung beans or sesame seeds in a small heavy skillet and dry-roast over medium-high heat, shaking constantly, until light brown and crisp, about 2 minutes. Remove from the heat. If using sesame seeds, pound briefly with a mortar and pestle or pulse in a mini-chop two or three times to release their flavor.

Ladle the warm bananas and tapioca into shallow bowls, sprinkle with the toasted mung beans or sesame seeds and serve with extra coconut milk on the side.

BUTTERCUP EGG CUSTARD
Sankiah L'poh

SERVES 8 TO 12

1 large buttercup squash (about 4 pounds)
1 or 1¼ cups unsweetened coconut milk
1 or 1¼ cups sugar
¼ teaspoon salt
5 or 6 large eggs

This is a most unusual and striking dessert: a large, round squash is cut like a cake into beautiful slices to reveal silky yellow custard surrounded by the deep orange flesh of the buttercup it is baked in. We used to call this one of our "Challenging Flavors" at The Elephant Walk, but it has become so popular that a cautionary note no longer seems necessary. The recipe is quite simple, although you do need to plan ahead, as it requires substantial cooking and cooling time.

Fill the bottom of a steamer with water and bring to a boil. Meanwhile, turn the squash upside down and cut a small hole in the bottom, about 2 inches in diameter (the top of the squash is now the base because it is the thickest part and will stay firm the longest). Reserve the plug. Scoop out the seeds and stringy insides with a spoon.

In order to find out how much custard the squash will hold, fill the squash with water up to the hole, then pour out and measure the water: there should be about 3 cups. If the squash holds much less, scoop out some of the flesh to make room for more custard; if the squash cavity is much bigger, you will need to use the larger amounts of coconut milk, sugar and egg indicated above, adding an extra pinch of salt.

Once the squash has been measured, double-wrap it in aluminum foil, leaving the foil open at the top.

In a small saucepan, heat the coconut milk until warm. Remove from heat and add the sugar and salt, stirring well to dissolve. In a medium bowl, beat the eggs with a fork or whisk until light yellow, about 30 seconds. Stir in the coconut milk mixture. Fill the squash with the custard mixture to nearly the top of the cavity, leaving a gap of an inch or two (the custard will rise a bit as it cooks, to fill the gap).

Put the wrapped squash on a plate, with the reserved plug next to it, and place the plate in the top part of the steamer. Cover and steam for 1½ hours, or until done. To test for doneness, insert a knife or chopstick into the custard: it should come out clean.

Cool for at least 3 hours before serving. If the squash has split in the course of cooking, it will tend to pull back together as it cools; press it gently at the fissure at intervals over the course of the cooling period.

Remove the aluminum foil from the squash.

Serve warm on a serving dish with the plug set alongside the whole squash. Slice into thin wedges.

SWEET RICE DUMPLINGS
Nom Plaiy Aiy

MAKES 25 TO 30 DUMPLINGS

8½ cups water
¼ pound palm sugar
1½ cups glutinous rice flour, or more if necessary
2 teaspoons sesame seeds
Pinch of salt
½ cup freshly grated coconut or packaged
    unsweetened shredded coconut

Everywhere on the streets of Phnom Penh, we used to be able to buy these wonderful little springy dumplings filled with palm sugar, which we would eat as a snack. At night, we'd get a craving for them and go down to one of the main thoroughfares, where women would be carrying baskets of them and calling out, *"Nom plaiy aiy,"* while their children tagged along behind. The sesame seeds and grated coconut sprinkled on top of these treats bring out the other flavors.

Put the water in a large pot and bring to a boil over high heat. Meanwhile, pinch off pieces of palm sugar and roll them into small balls, about ¾ inch in diameter; you should have 25 to 30. Set aside.

Remove ½ cup of the water from the pot. Put the 1½ cups rice flour in a small bowl and add the hot water a little at a time, mixing until a smooth dough forms. It should have the consistency of pie dough and should not stick to your hands (you can adjust the amounts of water and flour to get this right). Roll a rounded teaspoon of the dough into a ball and then flatten it into a circle (you will want to make the same number of rice flour circles as there are sugar balls). Place a ball of palm sugar in the center and wrap the rice dough around it, pinching it closed and rolling gently to smooth the edges (the resulting dumpling should be about 1¼ inches in diameter). Repeat with the remaining dough and palm sugar balls.

Add the dumplings to the boiling water, about a dozen at a time. They are cooked when they float to the top, 2 to 3 minutes. Remove with a slotted spoon and drain on paper towels.

Meanwhile, dry-roast the sesame seeds in a small heavy skillet over medium-high heat, shaking constantly, until light brown and crisp, about 2 minutes. Pound briefly with a mortar and pestle or pulse in a mini-chop two or three times to release their flavor. Mix the sesame seeds with the salt.

When the dumplings are all cooked, arrange them on a plate and sprinkle with the coconut and the sesame-seed mixture. Serve immediately.

SWEET PEA AND COCONUT PUDDING
B'baw Samdaik Ankoy

SERVES 4

9 cups water

½ cup black-eyed peas, soaked for several hours
    or overnight, drained

½ cup glutinous rice, rinsed

3½ cups unsweetened coconut milk, or more
    as needed, plus more for serving

⅔ cup sugar

½ teaspoon salt

When I was little and my mother made this pudding, I was always the first one at the table. I loved the combination of sticky rice and black-eyed peas with sweet, rich coconut milk, and even now, a warm bowl of it is heaven to me. Cambodians don't eat a lot of black-eyed peas, but when we do, it's in specialty desserts like this one. The peas require some time for soaking and softening, so you need to plan ahead.

Bring 5 cups of the water to a boil in a large saucepan and add the black-eyed peas. Return to a boil, reduce the heat to low and simmer until tender, about 1 hour (if you soaked the peas for the shorter time, you may have to increase the cooking time by 20 to 30 minutes). Drain.

Meanwhile, bring the remaining 4 cups water to a boil in a large saucepan. Add the rice, stirring constantly to keep it from sticking, and return to a boil. Reduce the heat to low and simmer, still stirring frequently, until the rice grains begin to split open and fall apart, about 15 minutes.

Add the coconut milk and black-eyed peas to the rice and simmer, stirring well, until the rice becomes mushy, 10 to 15 minutes (if the porridge is too thick, add more coconut milk). Add the sugar and salt and stir to dissolve. Serve warm or at room temperature, with more coconut milk on the side.

SWEET MUNG BEAN ROLLS
Nom Kruob Kanau

MAKES 30 TO 40 ROLLS

½ cup dried split mung beans, soaked overnight
   and drained
2 cups water
¼ cup unsweetened coconut milk
1 cup plus 3 tablespoons sugar
Pinch of salt
5 large egg yolks

Put the mung beans in a medium saucepan with ½ cup of the water and bring to a boil, stirring occasionally. Reduce the heat to low, cover and simmer until all the liquid has been absorbed, about 10 minutes. Remove any bean skins from the pot.

Increase the heat to medium-high. Add the coconut milk, 3 tablespoons of the sugar and the salt and cook, stirring and scraping constantly, until the beans become thick and begin to pull away from the sides of the pan, 7 to 8 minutes. Remove from the heat and allow to cool slightly.

Transfer the beans to a blender or food processor and puree until smooth and thick (if the mixture is too thin to be molded into rolls, return to the pan and cook until sufficiently thickened).

Meanwhile, press the yolks through a fine sieve set over a bowl by rubbing them back and forth gently with a spoon for several minutes. Set aside.

To prepare the syrup, put the remaining 1½ cups water in a medium saucepan, bring to a boil and add the remaining 1 cup sugar, stirring to dissolve. Return to a boil, reduce the

The name of this dish means, literally, "cake that looks like a jackfruit seed," and it is as charming to look at as it is delicious to eat. Tiny rolls of mung bean paste delicately flavored with coconut are dipped in egg yolks and cooked in a sweet, clear syrup. The mung beans require some advance preparation, and the dessert can be kept for several days, refrigerated, although you will want to be sure to allow the rolls to reach room temperature before serving. See the photograph on page 279.

heat to low and allow to simmer without stirring until the mixture thickens slightly.

Meanwhile, once the mung bean paste is cool enough to handle, roll out small amounts into little sausage shapes, about 1½ inches long and ¾ inch in diameter. In batches, dip the mung bean rolls into the prepared egg yolks to coat, then drop them into the simmering syrup, without crowding, and cook for about 2 minutes, turning once after about 1 minute. The egg coating will be opaque and shiny. Remove with a slotted spoon and serve warm or at room temperature.

GOLDEN ANGEL HAIR
Vawee

SERVES 4 TO 6

Looking for all the world like golden angel hair pasta, these brilliant strands of egg yolk glistening with sugar syrup are arranged on a plate and garnished with bright candied fruit. Only a few select shops in Phnom Penh ever offered sweets as fancy as this one, and they were made by women who had once lived in the Royal Palace. For me, the sight of this dessert always signals a most special occasion. The French, always appreciative of good desserts, love *Vawee*, but its origin is Thai, and before that, royal Khmer. You'll need a fine sieve and a funnel with a very narrow tube.

6 cups water
2 cups sugar
12 large egg yolks
1 teaspoon vanilla extract
Candied fruit (cherries or any other dried fruit that isn't yellow), for garnish

---

Bring the water to a boil in a large saucepan, add the sugar, stirring to dissolve. Return to a boil, reduce the heat to low and allow to simmer without stirring until the mixture thickens slightly.

Meanwhile, press the yolks through a fine sieve set over a bowl by rubbing them gently back and forth with a spoon for several minutes. Stir in the vanilla.

Pour some of the yolk mixture into a funnel with the smallest possible opening, covering the bottom hole with your finger. Moving the funnel in circles slightly smaller than the size of the pot, about 6 inches over the boiling sugar syrup, remove your finger from the hole and allow a thin stream to flow out as you circle the pan slowly three times, leaving a trail of egg yolks. Set the funnel aside and press down on the yolk strands in the syrup gently with a fork to ensure that they cook—they will turn a translucent yellow and will hold together when you move them—and then draw the fork across the pan to collect the strands into a hank. Hold the strands above the pan to allow some of the syrup to drip off, then place the strands on a plate to cool. (The process of cooking the strands should take only about 30 seconds). Continue with this process until you have used all the egg yolks.

To serve, gently tease out individual strands and pile them in the center of a dessert plate. Garnish with candied fruit and serve at room temperature.

GLOSSARY

ASIAN BANANAS are similar to the small yellow Hispanic variety and are sometimes called dwarf or finger bananas. They are slightly sweeter and more aromatic than the bananas Americans are most familiar with, which can be substituted. If using the larger bananas, cut them into smaller pieces.

ASIAN CHILI SAUCE is distinctive in its use of garlic and degree of sweetness. My favorite kind, which is called *sriracha,* is made from red serrano chili peppers. I buy it either imported from Thailand or made in California by Vietnamese.

ASIAN EGGPLANT, which are about the size and shape of golf balls, have a somewhat crunchy texture and a slightly bitter taste when eaten young and green. In Cambodian cooking, they are regularly served raw with dipping sauce or cooked in stews, where their bitterness is balanced by both sweet and salty flavors. You can use the large purple eggplant readily available in the supermarket produce section, but the smaller varieties that occasionally show up there make even better substitutes.

ASIAN FISH BALLS are available precooked in the refrigerator and freezer cases of most Asian markets. They need to be cooked only a short time, until they are heated through. Pieces of fish fillets can be substituted.

ASIAN LONG BEANS see *long beans.*

ASIAN NUTMEG can be found in the spice and seasoning section of any Asian market, both as a component of various mixed spices (see *five-spice powder*) or by itself. Somewhat softer than the nutmeg sold in this country, it grinds relatively easily in a blender. When making a spice paste, if you have only hard nut-

meg, grate it first before adding it to the blender. Mace is the thin covering that grows on the nutmeg, which can be purchased separately, usually in powdered form.

ASIAN SQUASH is a smooth, pale green vegetable that has the appearance of a slightly fattened zucchini, which serves as a good substitute. Asian squash should be peeled.

ASIAN TAPIOCA PEARLS, used as a thickener, are very small—about 1/16 inch in diameter. They can be found in Asian markets. Asian Best is a very common brand that offers several different sizes of pearls. I have also seen tapioca pearls in some health food stores and specialty markets. Larger pearl tapioca, available in regular grocery stores, can be substituted, although the cooking time required is longer.

BAMBOO SHOOTS are the cone-shaped new growth of the bamboo tree, cut when they are 6 to 12 inches long. To prepare them for cooking, peel away the leaves to reveal the off-white fibrous shoot, slice thinly and parboil for at least 5 minutes to soften and remove any bitterness. Fresh shoots have a much fresher taste and crisper texture, but I am not a stickler for using them. If you want to buy already processed bamboo, which is widely available both in cans and jars, trimmed and pre-cooked and packed in water, I recommend the canned whole shoots, sometimes labeled "bamboo shoot tips," rather than the sliced. Rinse them well before using. They will keep for 7 to 10 days after the can is opened if you change the water daily. Fresh and canned whole shoots are available in Asian markets.

BANANAS see *Asian bananas.*

BANANA BLOSSOMS are the compact purple heads from the tip end of the forming bunch, often about a foot long. Cambodians use them as a vegetable, primarily in salads but also in some noodle dishes. They are similar to artichokes in the texture of their uncooked leaves and the structure of their blossoms, and like artichokes they need to be soaked in lemon juice to keep them from darkening. Banana blossoms are prepared by removing the tough outer leaves and the underdeveloped "baby"

bananas inside; the more tender inner leaves are cut and sliced and held in acidulated water to keep from turning brown. The lovely purple ringlets have a mild, nutty flavor. Banana blossoms are available year-round in Southeast Asian markets and occasionally in Chinese markets.

BANANA LEAVES are regularly used as wrappers for steaming, and they impart a mild fragrance to the food inside. We also use these handsome dark green leaves as dishes, bowls and trays for serving food. You can buy frozen banana leaves in 1-pound bags in Asian markets; the ones you don't use can easily be refrozen and will keep almost indefinitely. To use frozen banana leaves, thaw them first, wipe them clean with a paper towel and cut away the tough center stem before wrapping food in them. If banana leaves are unavailable, substitute aluminum foil.

BASIL flavors are frequently used in Cambodian cooking, and many different herbs have a basil-like flavor. ASIAN BASIL (*chi ng'rong* or *chi krahom*) stems and flowers have a purple tinge, and its leaves are more pointed than those of regular sweet basil. HOLY BASIL (*mareh preuw)* is known for its slightly hairy leaves and a sweet clovelike aroma. It has a somewhat flat, mildly bitter taste that sweet basil only approximates, and it is used largely in stir-fries and sour soups. Both of these herbs are available in Asian markets, and Thai basil, as Asian basil is often called, is beginning to make an appearance in garden center herb sections. SIAM QUEEN is another variety being sold to gardeners. It is lighter green than sweet basil, with smaller, more pointed leaves and a flavor similar to that of Asian basil. All of these basils, including sweet basil, can be used interchangeably.

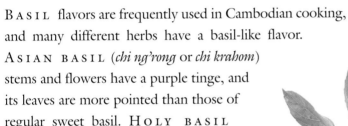

Asian Basil

Holy Basil

BEAN THREAD NOODLES, also known as bean thread vermicelli, cellophane noodles and glass noodles, are made from mung bean paste. Thin, shiny and transparent, they become opaque when soaked and cooked. The noodles, which come in handy 1¾-ounce packages (as well as larger ones), are used in soups and stir-fries and can be cut up into stuffing mixes.

To prepare bean thread noodles, soak them in warm water for 10 to 15 minutes. After that, the cooking time is literally a matter of seconds—just long enough to make sure that water has reached all the noodles. Rinse the noodles in cold water and drain.

BIRD'S EYE CHILIES (also known as bird peppers or Thai peppers; the name in Khmer is *m'teh k'mang* and in Thai, *prik kee nu*) have a sharp, piquant heat with a heady smell that lets you know what you're eating. They are ½ to 1 inch in length, and they start out light green and less hot when young and become darker, redder and hotter as they mature.

In most of the recipes, I have suggested using bird's eye chilies thinly sliced, but the traditional Cambodian method of eating them is to break one open with your spoon and scrape away at it a little at a time to release some flavor into each bite. Like fish sauce, bird's eye chilies are served in small bowls at every meal, so that each diner determines the spiciness of every individual dish (and, actually, of every spoonful).

These chilies keep in plastic bags in the refrigerator for close to a month (discarding any rotten ones as they appear increases the storage time of the lot). You can find them in stores pickled whole or you can make your own in a brine (page 258). I sometimes have to substitute serrano or jalapeño peppers or anything else from the local selection that is really hot, and occasionally even use the dried hot pepper flakes.

BITTER MELON is a relative of the cucumber. It has light to bright green skin, with warty bumps and ridges, and firm, green, bitter flesh that takes on a pinkish hue near the center when the fruit is more mature (this pink area has to be removed when the seeds are scooped out). Bitter melon can be also be found canned, but its flavor and texture suffer considerably.

Reminiscent of quinine, bitter melon is also used to ward off malaria. Its bitterness can be tamed somewhat by blanching or covering the melon with salt for 10 minutes and then rinsing, techniques that Westerners will probably want to try. Bitter melon adds a distinctive flavor to meats in particular, and it is usually combined in Khmer dishes with other strong seasonings, such as garlic and chilies. Sweetness is another good balancing complement, as in Stir-Fried Beef with Bitter Melon (page 116), which is a good introduction to a challenging, but wonderful, food.

BLACK-EYED PEAS look like small white pea beans with a black spot in the middle. Like *dried split mung beans*, black-eyed peas have to be soaked for several hours before they are cooked. They are mashed before being used in Cambodian recipes—usually desserts—where they provide a dry, slightly grainy texture.

BLACK FUNGUS, which is also known as wood ear, cloud ear, tree ear and—in Thai and Khmer—rat ear mushroom, is an edible wood fungus with a crunchy texture and a subtle, earthy flavor. Sold dried (in which form they last indefinitely), black fungi have to be soaked in warm water until they are soft and slippery and swollen to full size, about 15 minutes. (You may be surprised by how much they grow.) After soaking, check for dirt and cut out the hard stems.

In an Asian market, there are many different kinds and sizes of mushrooms marked "black fungus." Small tree fungi are ½ inch in diameter; 10 to 15 of them make ½ ounce. Large tree fungi are 1½ inches in diameter; 2 or 3 make ½ ounce. After soaking, the larger mushrooms should be cut into smaller pieces (½-inch squares) to resemble the small variety.

BUTTERCUP SQUASH, a large, round type of turban squash, not to be confused with the similar-sounding butternut squash, is used by Cambodians in some unfamiliar ways, most notably as a dessert.

CATFISH see *mudfish*.

CHAVAI see *rice stick noodles*.

CHAYOTE, a pear-shaped squash with light green skin, is enjoyed in soups, stir-fries and pickles. Although chayote is sweeter than *green papaya*, it can be substituted for it.

Chayote

CHILI PEPPER see *bird's eye chili, dried New Mexico chilies*.

CHILI SAUCE see *Asian chili sauce*.

Chinese Celery

Chinese Chives

Chive Blossoms

Chinese Red Dates

Chinese Sausage

Chinese Spinach

Chinese Watercress

CHINESE CELERY has thinner, deeper green stalks than its Western counterpart and a considerably stronger flavor. You can find it readily in any Asian market. Celery hearts may be substituted.

CHINESE CHIVES, which come tied together in a long bunch with their bulbs removed, look like their cousin, the scallion (which can be substituted), except that the leaves are flat. The CHIVE BLOSSOMS are purple when fully opened and are usually bundled and sold separately. They are best when the flower heads are mostly closed, along with their stems.

CHINESE RED DATES, also known as jujubes, look like plump dried cranberries and have a taste similar to prunes. Used often by the Chinese, these fruits appear less frequently in Cambodian cuisine, in some soups, stews and desserts.

CHINESE SAUSAGES look like hot dogs or long slender sausages, tied with rope. They are red with white patches of fat. They need to be cooked before being eaten.

CHINESE SPINACH, or water convolvus, which you can find in long bundles in Asian markets, has leaves shaped like arrowheads and a mild, tangy flavor that is particularly good in stir-fries and soups. The leaves can also be used to wrap small packets of food. Young flat spinach leaves can be substituted.

CHINESE WATERCRESS, sometimes under the name "green *ong toy*" in Chinatown, grows in freshwater streams and wet soil around the world and has a flavor similar, but not identical, to American watercress, which can be used in its place.

CHIVE BLOSSOMS see *Chinese chives*.

CILANTRO, or fresh coriander, is also known as Asian, Mexican or Chinese parsley because of its resemblance to the flat-leafed variety of that herb. Cambodians put only the stems in many of the spice pastes and use the leaves routinely as a garnish. In soups, cilantro should be added at the last moment so that its volatile, slightly musty flavor is not lost. Buy cilantro still attached to its roots whenever possible because it keeps far longer in this form.

COCONUT is actually only the seed, or nut, of the much larger fruit of the coconut palm tree. When this fruit is still green, the coconut is filled with a sweet juice that Cambodians prize (see *green coconut juice*).

Choose a coconut without any cracks or mold on the surface; it should slosh when you shake it, indicating that it is relatively fresh. To open a coconut, strike the shell sharply in a line around its middle until it breaks open (if you want to reserve the juice inside, drive a sharp tool such as an ice pick into one or two of the sunken "eyes" at one end of the shell and pour out the liquid before cracking open the shell). Break the shell into smaller pieces, pry off the outer husk and peel away the thin brown skin. The coconut meat is now ready to be grated. (See also *unsweetened coconut milk, unsweetened shredded coconut*.)

CORAL see *freshwater lobster*.

CUBANELLE PEPPERS are thin-skinned, light green peppers. Longer, thinner and less heavy than bell peppers, they only approximate the peppers used in Southeast Asia. They should be seeded but don't need peeling.

CUCUMBERS see *English cucumbers*.

CURRY LEAVES are sold in Indian markets or in Southeast Asian ones, where they are known as *sluk katrope*. In Southeast Asian markets, they are sold by the branch. The leaves are prepared by passing the branches back and forth over an open flame, toasting them until they crackle. At this point, the leaves will have a distinctive smoky flavor, slightly bitter. Break off the leaves by running your hand along the stem from bottom to top. In Indian markets, curry leaves are generally sold packaged, already stripped from the stems. Toast them in a dry pan until they crackle. There is no substitute for curry leaves.

DAIKON is a large white radish, 10 to 12 inches long, with a pungent, peppery taste. Daikon sweetens as it cooks, but it can also be eaten raw. Peel it before using. Firm, smooth roots taste best, but they do not store well. White turnips are an acceptable alternative. Daikon also comes pickled, sometimes marketed under the loose translation of "salted" or "preserved turnip." (See *preserved daikon*.)

DRIED LILIES, the unopened buds of the daylily, contribute texture and a mildly earthy fragrance to fried rice, salads, stews and soups. Imported from China, they can be found in any Asian market, usually in cellophane bags, and sometimes labeled "tiger lily buds." I prefer buds that are lighter brown in color and pliable, not brittle. Dried lilies store exceptionally well. Soak them in warm water for 10 to 15 minutes. The traditional practice of tying a knot in the middle of each bud holds the lilies together and makes them look more elegant.

DRIED LOTUS SEEDS, from the pale green fruit of the *lotus* plant, must be rehydrated by soaking in warm water. They add a wonderful nutty flavor to soups, stews and stuffings.

DRIED NEW MEXICO CHILIES, with their rich meaty flavor, make spice pastes red. They are very similar to the peppers used in Cambodia, but they retain their flavor much better when cooked in oil than do the bird's eye chilies that the Thai use for their red curry pastes. Dried chilies have to be soaked in warm water for about 10 minutes before blending them into a paste. Seed and devein them to keep the temperature mild and the texture smooth. One tablespoon of paprika can be substituted for each dried chili.

DRIED SHIITAKE MUSHROOMS are particularly prized by the Chinese (Chinese markets often have entire aisles devoted to them, some with staggering price tags). They have a strong, smoky taste. Shiitake mushrooms should be soaked in warm water for 10 minutes before using, longer if the soaking water is to be used for flavoring. The stems, which should be removed, are too tough to eat but are often added to a stockpot to lend extra flavor to a broth. These mushrooms keep indefinitely dried but last only a few days once soaked.

DRIED SHRIMP add an intense flavor to a variety of dishes. The shrimp are generally rinsed before being used whole or are soaked before being ground; they are then sprinkled over salads and noodle dishes and into stews. Dried shrimp are sold in clear cellophane packets, and I generally use the medium-sized ones (35 to 40 per ½ ounce). They should be brittle, not leathery, with a pinkish orange color and a lightly sweet smell.

DRIED SPLIT MUNG BEANS, which can generally be found in cellophane bags, range in color from white to pale yellow (whole mung beans, with skins on, are green). The cooking method and the end result are similar to those of *black-eyed peas*.

EGGPLANT see *Asian eggplant, pea eggplant*.

ENGLISH CUCUMBERS are less seedy and watery than their American cousins. This latter attribute is particularly important for salads, which shouldn't be too juicy. The skins of English cucumbers don't need to be peeled, only washed. When putting them in salads, score the skin lengthwise with a knife or fork so they absorb the flavors of the dressing.

FISH POWDER, a Thai product, is made from smoked fish and comes with and without chilies (I prefer the chili version). Fish powder can be found in any Asian market in glass bottles that look like spice jars.

FISH SAUCE appears in all the cuisines of Southeast Asia. Known as *tuk trey* in Cambodia (literally, "fish juice"), it is called *nuoc mam* in Vietnam and *nam pla* in Thailand. It is similar to Chinese soy sauce in the way it's made and used. Described in the simplest of terms, fish sauce is the liquid that is poured off from the fermenting *prahok* in a series of "pressings" (like those used to produce olive oil), with the first pressing being considered the best. Fish sauce does not need to be refrigerated.

For cooking, Squid brand fish sauce is very good. For an excellent dipping sauce, I recommend Phu Quoc brand, which comes from an island in Vietnam, where it is made from anchovies. Three Crabs Viet Huong brand is also a high-quality fish sauce for dipping and is less salty than most; it comes from Kampot Province in Cambodia. Sauces for spring rolls, salads and noodles (also called *tuk trey*) are made by adding such ingredients as garlic, ginger and lime juice to fish sauce; they will keep up to a month when refrigerated.

FIVE-SPICE POWDER is one of the best-known Asian spice blends. It usually includes powdered cinnamon, cloves, star anise, fennel seeds and either pepper or ginger. It is great in marinades and stews and also in vegetarian dishes, where it adds body. Five-spice powder can be found in many supermarkets, usually in the Asian products section. You can also find five-spice powder in different-sized cellophane bags in any Asian market, but buy it in small quantities because the spices lose their taste faster once they are ground.

Asian markets also carry cellophane bags of the same spices in whole form, labeled "assorted spices" and "seasoning materials." They include dried orange peel, licorice stem, cardamom seeds and nutmeg (see *Asian nutmeg*). This is a great way to buy a small quantity of a range of spices, and you can choose the mix that best suits your needs—if you are making a curry, for example—and fill in with any additional ingredients you need.

FRESH HAM, from the hind leg of the pig, is popular in Cambodian cooking because it is rich, flavorful and fatty. It is available in Asian markets in large, usually boneless, pieces. Western supermarkets and meat markets generally carry only the cured version. Pork tenderloin and pork loin are acceptable substitutes.

FRESHWATER LOBSTER (*b'kong*), also known by its French name, *langoustine,* has a relatively thin shell, long spindly legs and tiny front claws. These lobsters can usually be found in Southeast Asian markets in the freezer section, and, on occasion, fresh in regular fish markets and supermarkets (a phenomenon I suspect will become increasingly common). A single freshwater lobster has less meat than its saltwater cousin because it lacks the giant front claws, but the meat is so sweet that it more than makes up for quantity. After shelling lobsters, Cambodians routinely smash or slit open the larger of the front legs and use them to cook with because there is meat in them and plenty of flavor as well. In Cambodian etiquette, it is considered completely polite for people to suck on the shells to get at every last bit of meat—a technique I highly recommend.

Freshwater lobster is shelled and the stomach removed by cutting a small circle through the top shell just behind the eyes. The head is not removed. That's because one of the shellfish's favored features is found there: the oily pink sac that we call the coral, which, unlike the coral of saltwater lobsters, is not roe but fat. The coral is removed from the head after the lobster is cooked and stirred into the dish in quantities to taste. It has a strong, almost smoky quality and a lovely color. If the intestine running up the back of the freshwater lobster is dark, remove it as you would devein shrimp.

You can use saltwater lobster as a substitute for freshwater. Shrimp are also a good option, particularly jumbo shrimp, for any dish which includes large pieces of lobster meat. B L A C K T I G E R S H R I M P has a very nice color and a particularly good texture. Shell and devein them before using.

G A L A N G A L is also known as "greater galangal" (with "lesser galangal" being what I refer to in this book as *rhizome*). Cream-colored and resembling ginger, it has a more delicate, less biting flavor. Galangal, which can be found in Asian markets fresh or dried, is commonly used in Cambodian cooking, peeled and pounded into pastes. A single slice of galangal can also be used to give a nice roasted flavor to a dish. A thin slice the size of a quarter, coarsely chopped, is equal to about ¾ teaspoon. Some people think ginger is an acceptable substitute, but the flavors are different.

G A R L I C is used routinely in Cambodian spice pastes and stir-fries, and fried slices are often sprinkled over the top of a dish to finish it off. For the recipes in this book, assume that cloves are peeled and medium in size unless otherwise indicated. Seven medium cloves of garlic, coarsely chopped, yield about 3 tablespoons; 1 large head weighs about 2 ounces and contains 15 to 20 cloves. See also *pickled garlic*.

G I N G E R, with its pungent, aromatic flavor that is both hot and sweet, is considered by Asians a digestive aid, among its many other medicinal uses. Asian markets carry Y O U N G G I N G E R (mostly in frozen form), which has thin, light brown skin that does not need to be peeled. Mature gingerroot, which is available in Asian markets and most mainstream supermarkets, should always be peeled before using. The juice released from pounding slices of it can be used as a marinade to tenderize meat. Four ounces of julienned ginger equals approximately 1 cup.

GLUTINOUS RICE, also called sticky rice or sweet rice, has a higher starch content than long-grain rice, is creamy white with no translucence and holds together when cooked. You can find it in any Asian market. Buy it in small quantities unless you expect to make a lot of desserts.

To prepare glutinous rice for steaming, soak it in hot water to cover for at least 2 hours, preferably overnight. To cook, fill the bottom of a steamer with water and bring to the boil. Line the upper part of the steamer with a double layer of cheesecloth and spread out the soaked rice on the cloth. Put the cover on the pot and steam for about 15 minutes. The rice will get shiny as it cooks; it is done when there is no crunch left in the kernels when you bite into them. Let stand for 5 minutes before serving.

GLUTINOUS RICE FLOUR, finer in texture than ordinary *rice flour,* is used to make a dough that is soft and slightly chewy (see Sweet Rice Dumplings, page 274). There is no substitute for glutinous rice flour, and it is not interchangeable with ordinary rice flour. It can be purchased in Asian markets in 1-pound bags.

GRATED COCONUT see *unsweetened shredded coconut.*

GREEN COCONUT JUICE is the sweet aromatic liquid in the center of the unripened coconut, which we enjoy as a refreshing drink and also use to make fancy curries or *khar,* a sweetened kind of stew. The milky juice of a ripe coconut from the grocery store tastes only faintly similar, but it can be substituted if absolutely necessary. A better choice is green coconut juice from an Asian market, which comes frozen in clear plastic containers the size of a soda can. Second best is "coconut juice," which comes in soda cans in the same market. Both forms have some of the soft, unripened coconut meat, which is highly prized by Cambodians, mixed in.

GREEN PAPAYA, also known as pawpaw, is oval in shape and has a mild flavor and a pleasing crunchy texture. As the fruit

matures, the skin turns orange or yellow, the flesh around the mass of central seeds turns pinkish and the taste becomes sweeter. Like the *mango,* the green fruit contains an enzyme that tenderizes meat. *Jicama* and *chayote* can be substituted for green papaya.

JASMINE RICE is the preferred variety of rice in Cambodia. By rights, every recipe in this book, except for those calling for noodles, should end with the phrase "serve with rice," as that is what we normally do. Jasmine rice has a long grain and a delicate fragrance, not unlike basmati rice, which can be used in its place. It is served boiled and steamed with other dishes or eaten by itself. Jasmine rice is available in all Asian markets in a variety of sizes, from small bags to 50-pound sacks. Basmati rice is also available in these markets, as well as in many mainstream groceries. Other varieties of long-grain white rice can be substituted.

To cook jasmine rice: Some people believe in rinsing rice repeatedly before cooking, but I am not one of them; a quick rinse to clean the kernels is sufficient. The basic recipe for cooking rice is 1 cup of rice to 1¼ to 1½ cups of water, depending on the kind of rice, growing conditions and other factors. Put the rice and cold water in a pot and bring to the boil, then lower the heat and simmer, covered tightly, for 15 minutes. Let stand for another 10 minutes, still covered. (I generally allow 1 cup of uncooked rice per person, if they are Asian, or ½ cup for non-Asians.)

A surefire way to cook rice is to use an electric rice cooker or steamer, which not only cooks the rice but keeps it warm afterward. Rice cookers come in a wide range of sizes; 6-cup cookers sell for under $100. Rice cookers are available in Asian markets as well as most appliance and department stores.

JICAMA, which is also popular in Latin America, is a Southeast Asian tuber that resembles a brown turnip. It must be peeled before being used. It has a crisp, fresh taste that has been likened to something between an apple and a raw potato. In Cambodia, slices of jicama are often sprinkled with salt and pepper and eaten as a snack. Along with *chayote*, it is a good substitute for *green papaya*.

KAFFIR LIMES are small and warty, with a bitter rind and very sour juice. Cambodians use the rind and occasionally the whole fruit to achieve the fragrantly floral lime flavor we desire, but in this country, most Asian markets carry only the leaves. (Now that kaffir lime trees are being grown in California and Florida, this will probably change.)

KAFFIR LIME LEAVES are ground into spice pastes, used like bay leaves to flavor a broth or sliced into thin threads as a garnish. Dried kaffir lime leaves can also be used, but they have to be soaked for 10 to 15 minutes in warm water before being chopped and blended, and there is a substantial loss of flavor. Where fresh leaves are available, they are infinitely preferable, so buy lots of them at one time; they freeze very well, with no loss in flavor or color, and take up so little room. Before they are blended into pastes, fresh kaffir lime leaves should be deveined. A shortcut is to fold the leaves in half, dark sides together, and pull the vein up and away. I keep a bagful of already deveined kaffir lime leaves in the freezer.

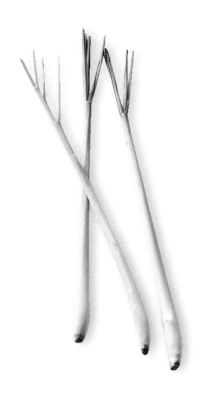

LEMONGRASS, one of the signature flavors of Khmer cuisine, provides a distinctively balmy lemon flavor that is reminiscent of its even more aromatic relative, citronella. In Cambodia, where it is used so often and thrives so well you see lemongrass growing in every garden. In this country, it can be found in any Asian grocery store—and increasingly in chain groceries, as well—sold in bunches.

Lemongrass resembles slightly dry, woody scallions, and like scallions, it is at its best when the tops of the leaves are still green. Lemongrass keeps for 2 to 3 weeks in the refrigerator but freezes even better, either whole or sliced. Dried lemongrass runs a very distant third because it has to be soaked in water until soft, is harder to cut and has less flavor.

Begin by cutting off the very bottom of the bulb of the fresh lemongrass and the top part of the stalk, leaving about 10 to 12 inches; remove any leaves that are brown or dried. Most of the recipes in this book call for lemongrass to be sliced thinly for spice paste, and a general rule of thumb is that 1 stalk, thinly sliced, yields about ½ cup. Slicing lemongrass can be a bit treacherous because the stalk is so tough; freezing fresh lemongrass breaks down the fibers some, making it easier to slice.

If the stalk is to be left whole, you will need to slit or smash the bulb to release its flavor, and the stalk should be removed before serving. Where more green coloring is desired in a dish, extra lemongrass leaves can be used. A soothing tea can also be made from lemongrass leaves.

There is no real substitute for lemongrass, although some people have tried the herb lemon balm and even lemon juice or lemon rind.

LIME see *kaffir limes, kaffir lime leaves, preserved limes.*

LOBSTER see *freshwater lobster.*

LONG BEANS, also called Asian long beans, Chinese beans and snake beans, are 12 to 16 inches long and sold in bunches in Asian markets. They are less sweet and more crunchy than their string bean relatives, which can be substituted. Because they retain their crispness when cooked, they are considered perfect for stir-fries.

LOTUS, a major symbol in Buddhism, representing the potential awakening of the eternal Self, grows in ponds and swamps throughout Cambodia. The plant is the source of many different foods. (See also *dried lotus seeds, lotus rootlets, lotus roots.*)

LOTUS ROOTLETS, which are the stems of the lotus plant, are sold in Cambodia in long bundles tied into big knots. Here, you will find them in glass jars in brine. With a texture and taste similar to asparagus, they are popular in soups.

LOTUS ROOTS have a fibrous flesh that is crunchy and sweet, like water chestnuts or *jicama,* both of which can be substituted, but starchier. Once peeled, they can be eaten raw or cooked.

LOTUS SEEDS see *dried lotus seeds.*

MA'AM is one of several Southeast Asian greens that add color and flavor to a dish. *Ma'am* has an almost cilantro-like taste, but sharper. Cilantro, basil or mint can be substituted.

MANGO is eaten unripe as well as ripe. When green, it is tart and crunchy and serves as a savory vegetable; it also contains enzymes that tenderize meat. The green fruit is usually used peeled and shredded or sliced into salads, and it is good in soups and ragouts too. Western supermarkets often won't put mangoes out when they are green and hard; Asian markets always have them.

MAREH PREUW see *basil*.

MINT is widely used in Cambodian cooking, but only a few varieties available in this country will taste right. FRENCH MINT (*chi barang* or *chi bonla*) has a saw-toothed leaf and a flavor somewhere between mint and basil. VIETNAMESE MINT is the kind most commonly sold in Asian markets, and it has long, tapering, aromatic leaves with a spearmint taste. KENTUCKY COLONEL, another kind of spearmint that has recently become available at garden centers, is even closer to the Cambodian original. Its leaves are almost round, not pointed like most American spearmints, which can be a little too strong and bitter, but which will do in a pinch.

French Mint

MUDFISH (*ruah*), a big fish with firm white flesh and a clean taste, is considered to be the best fish for grilling and a favorite in Cambodian cuisine generally. You can almost always find whole mudfish imported from Thailand in the freezer of a Southeast Asian market. CATFISH and TILAPIA are excellent freshwater substitutes, and RED SNAPPER and SEA BASS are acceptable saltwater stand-ins. Imported whole CATFISH (Asians don't fillet their fish) are sometimes also available in Southeast Asian markets, but be sure to get the kind with the yellow belly because this variety is known to live in clean water and its meat is particularly delicate.

MUNG BEANS see *dried split mung beans*.

MUNG BEAN SPROUTS are featured regularly in Cambodian salads and noodle dishes, as well as in stir-fries and soups. Off-white and a succulent source of vitamins, they are readily available in Asian markets and also, these days, in the produce section of Western supermarkets. Do not use canned sprouts.

Bean sprouts do not keep long, even when refrigerated. When cooking with them, add at the last minute to avoid overcooking.

MUSHROOM SOY SAUCE, like regular soy sauce, originates with Chinese cuisine and serves a purpose very similar to fish sauce in adding depth without overpowering other flavors. Mushroom soy sauce is darker, more full-bodied and less salty than regular soy sauce because of the addition of shiitake and straw mushrooms to its blend. In most recipes, you can replace mushroom soy sauce with what is called dark, or thick, soy sauce, but I would not use these in dipping sauces because they are too strong. Otherwise, regular soy sauce can be substituted.

MUSTARD GREENS can be found in many Western grocery stores, as well as in Chinatown and in Southeast Asian markets, where they also can be bought pickled. (See also *pickled mustard greens*.)

NEW MEXICO CHILIES see *dried New Mexico chilies*.

NUTMEG see *Asian nutmeg* and *five-spice powder.*

OLD WINTER MELON see *winter melon*.

PALM FRUIT, the fruit of the palmyra palm, from which *palm sugar* comes, is also known as "toddy palm's seed." It has a mildly nutty flavor, suggestive of coconut, and is used in desserts. Sold in this country packed in sugary syrup in cans or bottles, it keeps only a few days in the refrigerator once opened.

PALM SUGAR, which is not the same as coconut palm sugar or palm syrup, is made by tapping the sweet palm tree and then boiling down the sap until it is almost solid. In this country, palm sugar, which has a rich caramel taste, is sometimes sold in cakes but it also comes in plastic tubs, in which case it is generally soft enough to divide up with a spoon.

PAPAYA see *green papaya*.

PEA EGGPLANT grow in clusters and look like a cross between tiny green cherry tomatoes and hard green grapes. They

have a sprightly bitter taste, which Cambodians are particularly fond of, and can be cooked in stews, toasted and tossed into stir-fries or eaten raw with *prahok*-flavored dipping sauces. To reduce the bitterness, rinse the eggplants in salted water and boil briefly before using. There are no good substitutes for pea eggplant.

PEANUTS were introduced to Asia from the New World and were adapted quickly and broadly into the region's cuisines. They play especially major roles in Cambodian and Thai food. Roasted and usually coarsely ground, peanuts are sprinkled on top of many dishes, added to dipping sauces and salad dressings and sometimes used to thicken and enrich sauces. You can buy raw peanuts in and out of the shell at Western and Asian markets; they keep for a long time in the shell. Once they have been roasted and ground, however, they should be used within a week, or they turn stale or rancid.

To roast raw peanuts, put them in a pan in a preheated 350°F oven and cook, stirring occasionally to ensure even roasting, until golden brown, 10 to 15 minutes. Set aside to cool, when the nuts will harden again, then grind them—usually coarsely—with a mortar and pestle or in a mini-chop.

PICKLED GARLIC, which is both salty and sweet, is sold in cans and jars, packed in vinegar.

PICKLED MUSTARD GREENS (also called "sour mustard") are much better vacuum-packed than in canned form. (For a homemade version, see page 259.)

PICKLED SCALLIONS, sometimes called sugar scallions or pickled leeks, are usually found near pickled garlic in Asian grocery stores. They are actually small leek bulbs pickled in vinegar and sugar. They are sold in jars or cans.

PICKLED VEGETABLES can be served as snacks or side dishes. They come in a variety of forms and can all be found in Chinese and other Asian markets. (See also *pickled garlic, pickled mustard greens, pickled scallions.*)

POBLANO CHILI PEPPERS are greenish black in color and slightly heart-shaped, with a flavor similar to common varieties in Southeast Asia. They should be seeded but don't need peeling.

POMELO, the largest citrus fruit, is similar to a grapefruit in looks and taste but has a pulp that tends to be drier than regular grapefruit, so that the individual sections can be separated from the membranes without bursting.

PORK BELLY, called "five-flowered pork" by the Chinese in reference to its alternating layers of fat and meat, is a kind of Asian bacon; look for meaty pieces. Leaner *fresh ham* can be substituted. Cambodians leave the skin on pork belly, which adds more flavor, but this is a matter of personal taste. Leaner cuts like pork loin and tenderloin and fresh ham can be substituted.

PRAHOK, a gray, pasty preserved fish, is probably the most distinctive flavor in all of Cambodian cooking and certainly the most unusual for Westerners. Its smell has earned it the nickname "Cambodian cheese" in The Elephant Walk kitchen, and its odor is reminiscent of Limburger or ripe Camembert. You may ask why anyone would want to eat it (and a lot of Westerners have asked); the answer lies in something beyond flavor, which I can only describe as a kind of volume and body that a dish takes on as a result of the *prahok*.

Prahok is available in any Southeast Asian grocery store and usually in Chinese markets too (although they don't always stock the brands that I think are best). Labels sometimes read "fish sauce," which is a different product, and often refer to mudfish or "preserved gray featherback fish," as well. Be sure to buy *prahok* in glass jars, which allow you to check the quality of what you are getting. What you want to see is a grayish paste; there should be no chunks of fish discernible, nor any flour or roasted rice, as would be the case with some of the related fish-paste products that the Vietnamese make.

The imported Thai brands are generally what Cambodians buy, and I like one variety in particular that uses only the choicest fish and is known for its purity. It calls itself "*Siem Reap* style" (there's a drawing of Angkor Wat and Khmer letters on the label) to indicate that it is made in the Cambodian fashion, with all meat and no bones. Even if you have to search a bit, I recommend making the effort because that one jar of *prahok* will probably be all you need to buy in two or three years. And you do not need to keep it in the refrigerator.

A very small amount of *prahok* goes a long way, and it is usually cooked before being eaten (my husband, Ken, has tasted raw *prahok* only once in his life, and he didn't like it). Newcomers may want to use a light touch to start, adding additional *prahok* at the table and experimenting with increasing the amount over time. Some may want to dive right in and use the quantities I give in the recipes, while others, especially Cambodians, will probably double the amounts. It's all a matter of taste. There is really no substitute for *prahok*, although some people suggest using shrimp paste or anchovies in its place.

To make *prahok* juice, steep 2 tablespoons of *prahok* in ½ cup hot water for 5 to 10 minutes. Then, with the back of a spoon, press against the solids (you can also push them through a strainer) to extract as much of the juice and flavor as possible. Reserve the liquid and discard the solids. You can make a quantity of *prahok* juice and store it in a lidded jar in the refrigerator, where it will keep for several weeks.

PRAHOK JUICE see *prahok*.

PRESERVED CABBAGE, also called Tientsin or Tianjian preserved vegetables, comes in plastic tubs or ceramic pots—one of the greatest pottery bargains around. Extremely salty and slightly sweet, these shredded strips of grayish brown cabbage should be used sparingly.

PRESERVED DAIKON, also called salted or preserved turnip, has a warm taste and is both salty and slightly sweet. If it is too salty, it should be soaked in water before using. The best way to buy it is in vacuum-packed bags; it will be leathery looking and pale brown.

PRESERVED FISH products literally permeate the entire cuisine of Cambodia. While the smell is often quite pungent, what they add to the taste of a dish is saltiness and depth of flavor rather than a fishy taste. When cooking with preserved fish, be careful not to add it directly to a hot pan where there are no liquids, since the smell that results is quite noxious, even to devoted fans. (See also *prahok*.)

PRESERVED LIMES are sold in any Asian market in glass jars. Regular lime juice doesn't even approximate the flavor of preserved limes. There's really no substitute.

PRESSED BEAN CURD see *tofu*.

RHIZOMES, also known as lesser galangal and *krachai* in Thai, are tender, fingerlike roots with brown skins and yellow-orange flesh that are used most commonly in our spice pastes. When used fresh, they should be peeled first before being blended, but peeling is not necessary if they are frozen or pickled in brine, which are the most common ways you will find them in an Asian market. There is also a powdered form, which is adequate and stores very well. There are no substitutes for rhizome.

RICE see *jasmine rice*. See also *glutinous rice*, *glutinous rice flour*, *roasted rice powder*.

RICE FLOUR made from regular rice can be used as a thickener or to make *rice noodles* and *rice papers*. It can be purchased in Asian markets in 1-pound bags. (See also *glutinous rice flour*.)

RICE NOODLES are nearly as central to the Cambodian diet as rice, despite the fact that they are much newer to our table. These flat rice noodles, called *banh pho* by the Vietnamese, are Chinese in origin, not Khmer, which is why they are the only food that Cambodians eat with chopsticks. Rice noodles can always be bought in dried form, but on occasion you can also find them freshly made (like homemade pasta) in the cooler section of Asian markets. They are sometimes mistakenly labeled *rice stick noodles;* make sure you choose the flat product, shaped like linguine. I always buy rice noodles in the "small" size, which refers to the width.

   To prepare dried rice noodles for cooking, soak them in warm water for 10 to 15 minutes, then dip into boiling water, rinse in cold water and drain. Fresh noodles do not need to be soaked.

RICE PAPER SPRING ROLL WRAPPERS in Cambodian cooking are made with rice flour, unlike those used in Chi-

nese cooking, which are made with wheat flour. They come in a variety of sizes and shapes—circles, triangles and squares—and are used as wrappers and often fried. You can find rice paper wrappers in all Asian markets, usually in 12-ounce and 1-pound packages, both of which should be enough for a single recipe of spring rolls.

I find the triangular spring roll wrappers that are 6 inches to a side to be the easiest to use (Elephant Triangular is a popular brand); you can also buy round wrappers that are 12 inches in diameter and cut them into quarters after they have been soaked.

To prepare, dip the wrappers into warm water for a few seconds and then lay them out on a towel; they will become soft within a couple of minutes. Leftover dry wrappers should be tightly wrapped and stored, unrefrigerated, for later use.

RICE POWDER see *roasted rice powder*.

RICE STICK NOODLES are round, not flat like rice noodles, and are used in stir-fries, soups and salads. They come in a regular thickness and an extra-thin vermicelli in 1-pound rectangular bundles that look like cream-colored birds' nests. I like the Sailing Boat brand. (See *somen noodles* for an alternative to regular rice stick noodles.)

To prepare rice stick noodles, soak them first in warm water for 10 to 15 minutes. Drain and add them to boiling water, turn off the heat and let them stand for 15 minutes. Then rinse them under cold running water until cool and drain.

Serving-size bundles of rice stick noodles, called *chavai*, are made by looping handfuls of cooked noodles 8 to 10 inches long on a platter. The noodles will stiffen slightly and can be easily transported to a bowl of broth as needed.

ROASTED RICE POWDER is used to add flavor to a dish and to thicken sauces. To make it, wash uncooked rice first to plump it up (this makes the larger grains easier to grind), then toast it in a sauté pan over medium heat, stirring constantly to break up any clumps that form and to prevent burning. Remove from the heat when the darkest grains are a deep brown and the lightest ones are a pale gold (the entire process takes 5 to 8 minutes). Pound with a mortar and pestle or grind in a mini-chop until the rice is a fine powder. You can also buy rice already ground and roasted in Asian markets.

SALTED SOYBEANS add complexity to a dish. They come in cans and jars in Asian markets (I usually use Yeo's brand), and they are often available in the Chinese food section of mainstream supermarkets.

SHALLOTS are used liberally in Cambodian pastes, and we love slices of them fried until crisp and sprinkled on top of a dish as a final touch. One medium shallot is equal to 2 tablespoons coarsely chopped, and 1 large shallot, coarsely chopped, yields ¼ cup.

SHIITAKE see *dried mushrooms*.

SHRIMP see *freshwater lobster*.

SHRIMP PASTE (*kapih*) is made in a process similar to the one for *prahok* and has a strong fishy smell. Brown in color, it adds a pungent, salty flavor that is more concentrated than fish sauce. I prefer to use the Thai brands of shrimp paste that come in small jars because some of the other kinds, particularly those from China, tend to be thinner and have different textures and tastes (don't let the term "shrimp sauce" throw you—it's the same product). Shrimp paste is always added to a dish in small quantities, and it lasts virtually forever.

SLUK KATROPE see *curry leaves*.

SMOKED FISH POWDER see *fish powder*.

SOMEN NOODLES, made with wheat flour, are softer than *rice stick noodles* and can be substituted for them. The Japanese noodles, which actually look like sticks, usually come in 7- or 8-inch-long bundles tied with ribbon, packaged several bundles to a box. Do not soak Japanese noodles before cooking. Cook in boiling water for 1 to 2 minutes, or until tender, stirring with a fork to keep them from sticking. Drain, rinse and drain again.

SOY SAUCE see *mushroom soy sauce*.

SPICED DRY TOFU see *tofu*.

SQUASH see *Asian squash*, *buttercup squash*.

STICKY RICE see *glutinous rice*.

SWEET RICE see *glutinous rice*.

TAMARIND JUICE can be made by putting 2 tablespoons *tamarind paste* in ½ cup hot water and allowing it to steep for 5 to 10 minutes. With the back of a spoon, press against the solids—you can also use a strainer—to extract as much of the juice and flavor as possible. Reserve the liquid and discard the solids. You can make a quantity and store it in a jar in the refrigerator, where it will keep for several weeks. Lime juice can be substituted for tamarind juice.

TAMARIND PASTE is the dark pulp from the inside of the flat, beanlike pods that grow on giant tamarind trees. From an Arabic word for "Indian date," tamarind was introduced to the region by Indian traders. Cambodians use tamarind to darken soups and curry sauces and to give them a sour, slightly sweet taste. You can find soft, pliable blocks of tamarind, with or without seeds, in Asian and Indian markets. Knorr makes a powdered Tamarind Soup Base Mix, which is very handy. Tamarind liquid, called "pure fresh tamarind" or "liquid tamarind concentrate," is sold in cans in Asian markets—all of these are acceptable.

TILAPIA see *mudfish*.

TOFU, made from soybean curd, is used in moderation in Cambodian cooking, primarily in stir-fries, which are Chinese in origin. The two kinds I recommend are PRESSED BEAN CURD and SPICED DRY TOFU, which are drier and firmer than the fresh tofu you buy in tubs in the supermarket and hold up well during vigorous stir-frying. Both are light to medium brown in color, and their flavors are mild enough not to compete with their companion ingredients. They can be found in the refrigerated section of any Asian market, usually vacuum-packed. (Be sure not to buy "salted bean curd," which has the right texture but is much too salty.)

Fresh tofu—even extra-firm—tends to disintegrate when stir-fried, but you can firm it up somewhat, if you need to, by deep-frying slices of fresh tofu before cubing them; be careful to toss them gently during stir-frying.

TUK TREY see *fish sauce*.

UNSWEETENED COCONUT MILK entered Cambodian cuisine (and Thai cuisine) by way of Java and the Indonesian nobility. Do not confuse this product with *green coconut juice* or with the highly sweetened "coconut cream" sold for use in rum drinks like piña coladas.

Canned unsweetened coconut milk is readily available in Asian markets. My favorite brand is Mae Ploy, which comes in 19-ounce cans. Chaokoh, found in smaller cans, is also very good, and most of the other brands from Southeast Asia are acceptable. The Thai brands that have been Westernized for the chain supermarkets are distant runners-up, but the Latino "creams" are too sweet and should be avoided altogether. When you open a can of coconut milk, be sure to mix the milk well with a spoon, as the thicker cream tends to rise to the top of the can. Once opened, coconut milk keeps when refrigerated for about 10 days.

To make coconut milk at home, cover 2 cups of freshly grated (or desiccated) coconut with 2½ cups very hot water and let steep for 30 minutes. Blend in the blender, pulsing a few times to make it a mush (this step allows you to extract more milk). Pour the coconut through a strainer lined with cheese-cloth, squeezing the cloth to get as much milk as possible (there should be at least 2 cups).

Coconut milk has a high fat content and is very rich, and even in Cambodia, the dishes that feature it are not considered everyday offerings. For those concerned about fat, there are some low-fat versions on the market, and it is also possible to halve the quantity of coconut milk called for and add water to make up the difference. Coconut extract, available in some supermarkets and at specialty food markets and gourmet shops, can be added to milk (½ teaspoon to 1 cup milk) to reduce the fat content even further. (Keep in mind that all of these lack the body, richness and flavor of the original.)

When using coconut milk in a curry, the trick is to heat it until the coconut oil separates from the milk, 2 to 3 minutes. This oil is used to cook the curry spices, and if the oil has not separated before the spices are added, their tastes will be muddy.

UNSWEETENED SHREDDED COCONUT can be made fresh or bought. Freshly grated is tastier than either desiccated or frozen shredded coconut. Open the coconut (see *coconut*), reserving the juice, and prepare the meat by prying off the outer husk and peeling away the thin brown skin. Grate the coconut meat with a sheet grater, box grater or mandoline, or process in a blender, food processor or mini-chop.

You can usually find desiccated grated coconut (called, simply, shredded coconut) in plastic bags in Asian markets and in health food stores and near it, a more moist variety. Both kinds can be used without any soaking. You can also sometimes find it frozen. Be careful not to buy your coconut meat sweetened, which is the way it is often sold in Western supermarkets; that kind is intended for baking.

WINTER MELON, when allowed to mature, is one of the world's largest vegetables, growing to several feet long and weighing up to 100 pounds, though it is usually sold cut into individual pieces. Sometimes known as wax gourd, it has a thin, green, waxy skin like that of a watermelon, and it must be peeled. OLD WINTER MELON is most popularly used to make a clear soup during the summer, since it is supposed to cool down the body. YOUNG WINTER MELON is picked at 10 to 12 inches long and has a softer texture and a milder taste. It is served steamed, braised, parboiled or stir-fried. Whole winter melon keeps sometimes for months; once peeled and cut, it lasts for about a week.

YOUNG GINGER see *ginger*.

YOUNG WINTER MELON see *winter melon*.

YUCA, or cassava, is a root vegetable that looks like a dark sweet potato and is the source of tapioca. It has a bland, starchy, slightly sweet and buttery taste, which makes it perfect for serving with more highly flavored sauces. Select yuca without mold or cracks in the very thick, waxy skin, which has to be slit and then peeled off like bark from a tree before cooking. The insides of the yuca should be very white and not spotted. Raw yuca does not store well, so be prepared to use it in a timely fashion.

SOURCES

Wherever there are Asian people living in this country, you will find Asian markets. The older established markets tend to be Chinese, the more recent ones Thai because it is the Thai who have taken the lead in exporting food products to this country and worldwide. Some of the markets call themselves Southeast Asian markets, catering to the needs and tastes of a variety of different Asian communities. In areas like Boston and Long Beach, California, where significant numbers of Cambodians live, there are even specifically Cambodian stores. The Elephant Walk in Cambridge, Massachusetts, stocks all the ingredients used in the recipes in this book as well as a variety of Cambodian artifacts, including silks, jewelry and handcrafts.

Even if you live far from these corner groceries, however, you can obtain most of the necessary ingredients through a variety of mail-order businesses. Here is a list of sources to get you started. You may also want to check your phone book for additional Asian markets in your area.

Balducci's
95 Sherwood Avenue
Farmingdale, NY 11735
(800) 225-3822

The Cook's Garden
(for gardeners)
P.O. Box 65
Londonderry, VT 05148
(802) 824-3400

Dean & DeLuca
560 Broadway
New York, NY 10012
(800) 221-7714; in NYC (212) 431-1691

DeWildt Imports
Fox Gap Road, R.D. 3
Bangor, PA 18013
(800) 338-3433; in PA (215) 588-0600

The Elephant Walk Marketplace
2067 Massachusetts Avenue
Cambridge, MA 02140
(617) 492-6900
www.elephantwalk.com

Kalustyan
123 Lexington Avenue
New York, NY 10016
(212) 685-3451

Oriental Pantry
423 Great Road
Acton, MA 01720
(800) 828-0368
Fax (781) 275-4506

Pacific Mercantile Company
1925 Lawrence Street
Denver, CO 80202
(303) 295-0293
Fax (303) 295-2753

Rafal Spice Company
2521 Russell Street
Detroit, MI 48207
(800) 228-4276; in MI (313) 259-6373

SoHo Provision
518 Broadway
New York, NY 10012
(800) 450-8987; in NYC (212) 334-4311

The Spice Merchant
P.O. Box 524
Jackson Hole, WY 83001
(800) 551-5999

Sweetwater Aqua Farms
(for freshwater prawns)
Adam Road and State Route 510
San Benito, TX 78586
(800) 477-2967
Fax (212) 579-9092

Uwajimaya
519 Sixth Avenue South
Seattle, WA 98104
(800) 889-1928
Fax (206) 624-6915

INDEX

Page numbers in *italics*
refer to illustrations.

C

as substitute for winter melon, 100
substitutions for, 131, 284
Squid Brand fish sauce, 291
Sriracha brand chili sauce, 283
Sticky rice
about, 294
with Palm Fruit, 268
Topped with Shellfish, 65–66, 67
Stir-fried dishes. *See also* Rice: fried
Beef, Spicy, 114–15
Beef with Bitter Melon, 116
Beef with Chinese Celery, 108, 109
Beef with Lemongrass, 112–13
Beef with Pineapple, 110
Beef with Tomatoes, 111
Buttercup Squash with Pork, 132, 133
Catfish, Ginger, 157
Chicken with Ginger, Onions, and Scallions, 191
Eggplant and Pork, 130
Green Squash with Pork, 131
Pork with Bean Sprouts, 129
Pork with Long Beans, 128
Pork with Onions, 127
Shrimp with Snow Peas, Stir-Fried, 174, 175
Street food
Beef, Grilled, with Lemongrass Paste, 53–54
Beef with Eggplant in Coconut Milk, 117–19, 118
Chicken Wings, Spicy, 56–57
Corn, Grilled, 62
Noodle Soup, Classic, 78–80, 81
Pork Brochettes with Shredded Coconut, 58, 59
Spring Rolls, Cambodian, 46–48, 47
Substitutions, of ingredients
for catfish, 166
for Chinese watercress, 90
for curry leaves, 289
for daikon, 289
for galangal, 293
for green papaya, 237, 294, 295
for lemongrass, 296
for lobster, 99, 174, 292–93
for *ma'am*, 297
for mudfish, 298
for pomfret, 162
for pork belly, 300–301
for *prahok*, 301–2
for rice stick noodles, 305

for squash, 131, 284
for watercress, 90
for winter melon, 100
Sugar scallions, about, 300
Sweet rice. *See* Sticky rice

T

Tamarind juice
Beef Curry, Braised, with Peanuts, 122–23
Beef Stew, Sweet, 120–21
Catfish, Curried, 166–67
Chicken Soup with Eggplant, Khmer, 86, 87–88
to make, 306
Papaya Salad, Green, 237
Pork, Ginger, with Peanuts, 43–44, 45
Pork Soup, Lemongrass, 90–91
Pork with Peanuts, Ginger, 43–44
Sour Soup with Beef, Cambodian, 92–93
Sour Soup with Coconut Milk and Pineapple, 94–95
Sour Soup with Tomato and Lotus, 96, 97–98
Vegetables, Fresh, with Dipping Sauce, 246–47
White Fish Soup with Young Winter Melon, 100–101
Tamarind paste, about, 306
Tamarind Soup Base Mix brand, about, 306
Tapioca pearls, about, 284
Three Crabs Brand Viet Huong fish sauce, 291
Tianjian preserved vegetables, 302
Tientsin preserved vegetables, 302
Tiger lily buds. *See* Lilies, dried
Tilapia, as substitute for mudfish, 298
Toddy palm's seed. *See* Palm fruit
Tofu
about, 306–307
Pork, Stir-Fried, with Chive Blossoms and, 134
Pork with Bean Sprouts, 129
salted bean curd, about, 306
Tomato(es)
Bean Sprouts, Pickled, with, 254
Beef, Stir-Fried, with, 111
Beef, Stir-Fried, with Chinese Celery, 108, 109
Chicken, Steamed, 187
Relish, 252

V

W

Y

Z